TRAVELLERS

ESTONIA

By
ROBIN GAULDIE

Written and updated by Robin Gauldie
Original photography by Robin McKelvie

Published by Thomas Cook Publishing
A division of Thomas Cook Tour Operations Limited
Company registration no. 1450464 England
The Thomas Cook Business Park, 9 Coningsby Road,
Peterborough PE3 8SB, United Kingdom
E-mail: sales@thomascook.com, Tel: +44 (0) 1733 416477
www.thomascookpublishing.com

Produced by Cambridge Publishing Management Limited
Burr Elm Court, Main Street, Caldecote CB23 7NU

ISBN: 978-1-84157-899-6

Series Editor: Maisie Fitzpatrick
Production/DTP: Steven Collins

Printed and bound in Italy by Printer Trento

Cover photography: Front: L-R: © Jon Hicks/Corbis, © MedioImages/Getty Images; © Jon Hicks/Corbis. Back: L-R: © Schmid Reinhard/SIME-4Corners Images; © World Pictures/Photoshot.

The paper used for this book has been independently certified as having been sourced from well-managed forests and recycled wood or fibre according to the rules of the Forest Stewardship Council.
This book has been printed and bound in Italy by Printer Trento S.r.l., an FSC certified company for printing books on FSC mixed paper in compliance with the chain of custody and on products labelling standards.

Contents

Introduction

Estonia is one of Europe's smaller countries. To visitors, it offers a fascinating history, a lively, youthful culture and a surprising variety of landscapes: from thick forests that shelter elk, bear, wolf and wild boar, to Baltic beaches and offshore islands. A wealth of historic towns, castles, cathedrals and aristocratic mansions waits to be explored. Less than two decades after independence from the former USSR, Estonia is an exciting place as it comes into fully fledged nationhood, emerging from a turbulent history.

Membership of the European Union, which it acquired in 2004, has given Estonia a sense of belonging – voluntarily – to a greater cultural and economic identity. Estonia's language is closely related to Finnish, and so Estonians feel culturally closer to their Finnish neighbours across the Baltic Sea than to neighbours in Latvia, the small former Soviet Baltic republic on the southern border. They feel even less affinity with their big eastern neighbour, Russia, which occupied Estonia for centuries. There is still considerable hostility towards the country's Russian-speaking minority.

Estonians have a reputation for being rather aloof, but this is unjustified. This is not a culture given to spontaneous displays of wild abandon, but in general Estonians are friendly and very helpful to visitors, and English is very widely spoken.

Tallinn

Since the lifting of the Soviet yoke, Estonia's lively and picturesque capital, Tallinn, has metamorphosed into one of Europe's most popular short-break destinations. It has also attracted a number of young expatriates, drawn by its low cost of living, exuberant culture and new business opportunities.

Tallinn has an excellent and varied choice of good hotels and cosmopolitan restaurants, and new places to stay, eat and drink are opening all the time. There are also plenty of good places to eat and drink in Tartu, Pärnu and other regional towns and cities such as Narva and Kuressaare.

Tallinn attracts crowds of youthful fun-seekers. It also draws its share of visitors keen to experience its remarkable heritage of medieval architecture. Relatively few visitors venture far beyond the capital, but Estonia's small size makes it easy to explore even on a short break. To the historically inclined, it offers a rich reward of ancient towns and medieval castles.

Its beautiful lakes, clear rivers and thick pine forests are views no visitor would want to miss; islands dotted with fishing communities and visited by huge flocks of migrant sea birds make Estonia a unique getaway.

For many people, the nightlife of Tallinn is a major attraction. But the country's wide-open spaces also offer a range of open-air activities: from canoeing and rafting on lakes and rivers, sailing and other water sports on the Baltic coast, to wildlife viewing and cycling on forest trails.

As a northern European country in the same northern latitudes as St Petersburg and southern Scandinavia, Estonia has long, light summer evenings that make it perfect for sightseeing, or for an active holiday exploring its beautiful hinterland.

Winter days are short and chilly but have a beauty all their own – snow covers fields and forests, and there is ice on the lakes, the rivers and the Baltic Sea.

A view of Tallinn

The land

Estonia is located on the south shore of the Gulf of Finland, at the eastern end of the Baltic Sea, at latitude 59° north and longitude 26° east. It covers a land area of 45,226sq km (17,462sq miles).

The climate

The climate is maritime and wet, with moderately cold winters and cool summers. The influence of the Baltic Sea moderates winter temperatures, which may be a few degrees warmer on the coast than inland. Winter temperatures from November to March hover around freezing, with daytime temperatures rising to no more than 4°C (39°F) and snow cover for up to five months of the year inland. In summer, maximum daytime temperature is normally around 22°C (72°F) but occasionally temperatures can rise to 27–28°C (81–82°F).

Estonian wild campanulas

The shallow offshore waters may freeze in winter, but long summer hours of sunshine (with 19 hours of daylight at midsummer) make the Baltic waters surprisingly warm in July and August and pleasant for swimming. Rainfall is around 600mm (24in) per year, with around 150mm (6in) of precipitation falling as snow.

Lakes and forests

Estonia – like its neighbours – is a low-lying country, with its highest point, the summit of Suur Munamägi, rising to just 318m (just over 1000ft) above sea level. The terrain is marshy and heavily forested, with woodland covering around 44 per cent and only 16 per cent of the

Estonia

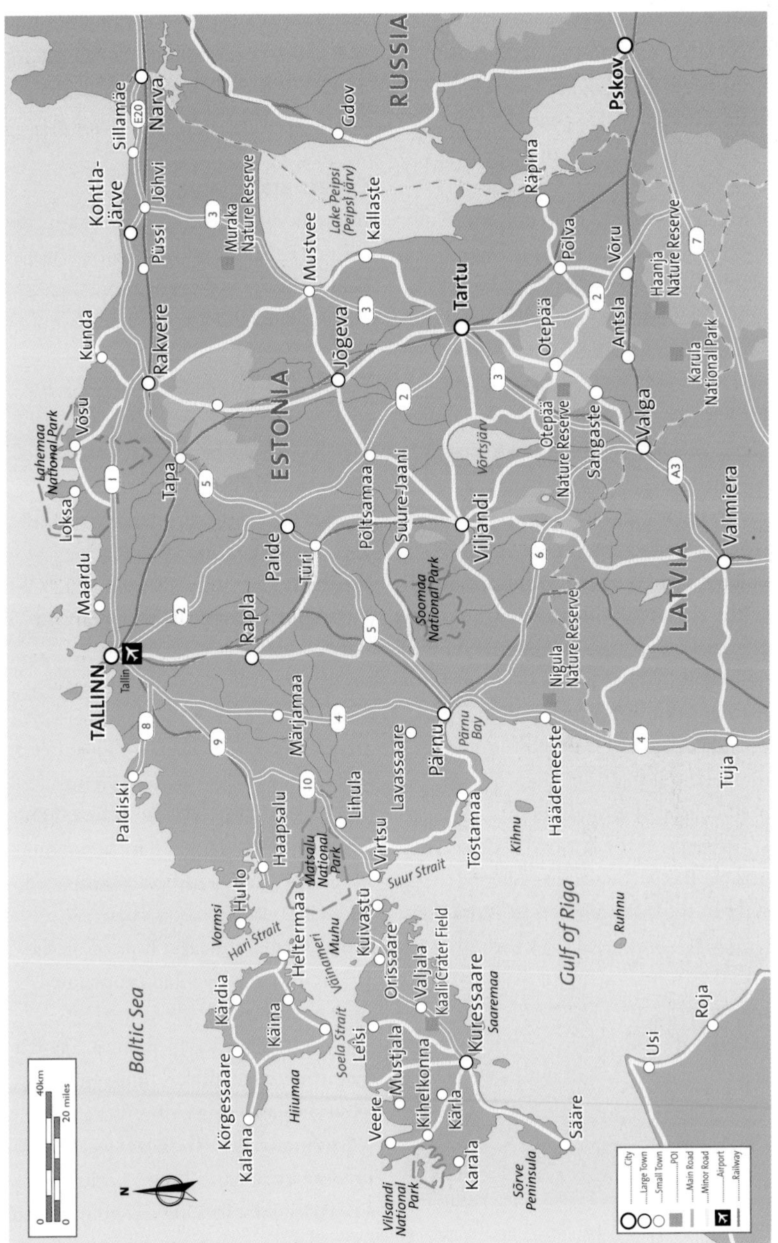
RUSSIA
ESTONIA
LATVIA
Baltic Sea
Gulf of Riga
Lake Peipsi (Peipsi järv)
Võrtsjärv
Pärnu Bay
Suur Strait
Hari Strait
Soela Strait
Väinameri
TALLINN
Tallinn
Tartu
Pskov
Narva
Sillamäe
E20
Kohtla-Järve
Jõhvi
Püssi
Kunda
Rakvere
Võsu
Loksa
Maardu
Lahemaa National Park
Muraka Nature Reserve
Gdov
Mustvee
Kallaste
Räpina
Põlva
Võru
Haanja Nature Reserve
Jõgeva
Otepää
Otepää Nature Reserve
Antsla
Karula National Park
Sangaste
Valga
Valmiera
A3
Tapa
Paide
Türi
Põltsamaa
Suure-Jaani
Viljandi
Soomaa National Park
Nigula Nature Reserve
Rapla
Märjamaa
Pärnu
Lavassaare
Häädemeeste
Tüja
Paldiski
Haapsalu
Lihula
Virtsu
Matsalu National Park
Tõstamaa
Kihnu
Ruhnu
Vormsi
Hullo
Heltermaa
Kärdia
Käina
Kõrgessaare
Kalana
Hiiumaa
Muhu
Kuivastu
Orissaare
Valjala
Kaali Crater Field
Leisi
Mustjala
Kihelkonna
Kärla
Veere
Karala
Kuressaare
Saaremaa
Sääre
Sõrve Peninsula
Vilsandi National Park
Roja
Usi
1
2
3
4
5
6
7
8
9
10
0
40km
20 miles
N
City
Large Town
Small Town
POI
Main Road
Minor Road
Airport
Railway

country under arable farmland. Lakes – around 1,400 of them, ranging from small forest pools to Peipsi, which is the fourth largest lake in Europe with a surface area of 3,555sq km (1,373sq miles) – dominate the countryside. Estonia's frontier with Russia runs through Lake Peipsi from north to south, and follows the course of the River Narva, which rises from Lake Peipsi to flow north into the Gulf of Finland. Lake Võrtsjärv, in the south of the country, covers some 270sq km (104sq miles). Estonia's lakes are shallow: Peipsi is only 15m (49ft) at its deepest, and Võrtsjärv is less than 6m (20ft) deep.

Marshland, including deep peat bogs, cover more than 20 per cent of the country. Peat is one of Tallinn's natural resources, along with oil shale, but both are mixed blessings. Peat extraction is a potential threat to Estonia's unique natural environment, and sulphur dioxide emissions from power plants that burn oil shale for fuel have been a major cause of air pollution.

However, in the last two decades, Estonia has succeeded in reducing sulphur dioxide pollution by more than 80 per cent and reducing waste-water pollution to less than 5 per cent of mid-1980s levels. Since the end of Soviet domination, there has been a greater awareness of environmental issues.

Wildflower meadow near Pärnu

Coasts and islands

Estonia's coastlines face north, across the Gulf of Finland, and west, across the Gulf of Rīga. Offshore lie more than 1,500 islands and islets, ranging from larger isles such as Saaremaa and Hiiumaa to dots on the map like Kihnu, Ruhnu and even tinier skerries. Most of these islands are barren and uninhabited, partly because access to them was banned during the decades of Soviet rule.

Wildlife

Environmental awareness, sadly, does not yet extend to offering full protection to Estonia's forest wildlife. The country's thick woodlands – which are mainly coniferous, with some beech and birch woods – shelter as many as 500 brown bear, 100–150 wolves, 700 lynx (by far the largest lynx population in Europe) and many thousands of elk and wild boar. Raccoon dogs, introduced as fur-farm inmates in the 1950s, have escaped and proliferated. All are enthusiastically hunted by Estonians. Since independence, Estonia has attracted wealthy hunters from western Europe and America.

Estonian lakes, rivers and forests also provide a home for beavers, flying squirrels and a handful of species including raccoons, muskrat and mink, which were introduced from North America during the Soviet era, when they were farmed for their fur.

More than a dozen species of rare frogs, newts and salamanders are found here, and spectacular bird species include endangered golden eagles: Estonia shelters around 250 breeding pairs.

Despite its northerly climate and chilly winters, Estonia's rich soil fosters almost 1,500 plant species, from conifers such as pine, fir and the mighty larch, to cold-tolerant deciduous trees such as birch, elder, lime and beech. The marshy wetlands are home to numerous orchids.

Population and people

Estonia has a population of around 1,333,000, with around 400,000 people living in Tallinn, the capital and the only large city. Large towns include Tartu, with a population of 101,000; Narva (69,000); Kohtla-Järve (48,000) and Pärnu (46,000). Overall population density is low, with only 30 people per square kilometre.

Just under 70 per cent of Estonian citizens are ethnic Estonians, with ethnic Russians accounting for more than 25 per cent of the country's residents (in Tallinn, more than 40 per cent are ethnic Russians). Other minorities include small numbers of Ukrainians, Belarusians and Finns. Although most were born and brought up in Estonia, and many are the descendants of Russians who settled here generations ago, their presence is a

The Russian influence can still be seen in Estonia

constant reminder of Russian dominance and is still resented by many Estonians. On the other hand, many ethnic Russians feel that they have been excluded from the opportunities and benefits of the new Estonia. Most ethnic Russians have chosen to become Estonian citizens, but a requirement for citizenship of the new Estonia is knowledge of the Estonian language and the official new version of the country's history. Many older Russian-speakers feel unable to meet these requirements, and as a result, some 165,000 ethnic Russian former Soviet citizens in Estonia are technically stateless and disenfranchised.

Christianity came late to pagan Estonia, which was forcibly converted during the 13th century and adopted the Lutheran Protestant faith in the 17th century. Organised religion was frowned upon during the Soviet occupation. As a result, only around 32 per cent of Estonians – including 180,000 Lutherans and 170,000 Russian Orthodox worshippers – claim any religious affiliation, and there is no state-sponsored faith.

History

9000–7500 BC	First signs of human settlement in the region of modern-day Estonia, including stone tools and weapons.
3000–2000 BC	Finno-Ugric tribes, of whom descended today's Estonians, Finns, Sami and Karelians, migrate from the east and settle around the Gulf of Finland.
AD 1202–30	Knights of the Sword, an order of Germanic crusaders, conquer most of Estonia and Latvia, defeating the Estonian chieftain Lembitu (Lembit) in 1217, and forcibly convert their people to Christianity. Denmark seizes Reval (later known as Tallinn) and northern Estonia, but cedes it to the Knights of the Sword in 1227. At this time, and until independence, Estonia is part of a region known as Livonia, which also includes a part of present-day Latvia.
1242	Russian Prince Alexandr Nevsky defeats Teutonic Knights at Lake Peipsi, ending their 'drang nach osten' (drive to the east).
1343–46	St George's Night Rising against Danish rule in northern Estonia. Denmark sells the region to the Livonian Order of Teutonic Knights, giving them control of most of Estonia. German barons dominate the country until the 20th century. Merchants of the Germanic Hanseatic League control coastal commerce and towns including Reval and Pärnu.
1558–1629	The Baltic states are ravaged by the Livonian Wars, involving Muscovy (Russia), Sweden and Poland-Lithuania.
1582	Poland-Lithuania finally drive Muscovites (Russians) from southern Estonia. Sweden drives Muscovites out of northern and western Estonia. Denmark seizes Saaremaa island.
1592–1629	War between Sweden and Poland. Sweden drives

	Poland from Livonia and converts the region from Roman Catholicism to the Lutheran Church.
1645	Sweden acquires Saaremaa island from Denmark.
1700–21	Great Northern War between Russia and Sweden ends in Swedish defeat. By the Treaty of Nystad 1721, Russia acquires Estonia and Latvia.
1800–1900	The 19th century is a relatively peaceful era for Estonia. It remains untouched by the French Revolution and Napoleonic Wars (1789–1815). Baltic-German barons and landowners continue to control the country under Russian rule. Starting in 1811, Estonian serfs – peasants who were virtually the chattels of the landowners – are freed and allowed to own land of their own. Education flourishes, and in the latter 19th century Tartu University (founded during the Swedish era) becomes a centre of learning and Estonian national culture, while Reval and Narva grow into industrial cities. The Lutheran faith encourages literacy, and by the end of the century, almost all Estonians can read. A Reval–St Petersburg railway opens in the 1890s.
1914–18	As part of Russia, Estonia is drawn into World War I on the Allied side and is briefly occupied by Germany.
February 1917	First Russian Revolution overthrows the monarchy. New Russian government grants Estonia self-government under Russian rule.
February 1918	Germany invades Estonia. Estonia declares full independence from Russia. Tallinn (as Reval is now to be known) is occupied by German troops. With the defeat of Germany in November 1918, Soviet Russia attempts to reconquer Estonia (as well as Latvia and Lithuania) but fails due to British military and naval intervention.
1919	The last Red Army troops are expelled from Estonian soil in February 1919.

1920	Soviet Russia signs treaty formally recognising Estonia as an independent state, ushering in two decades of independence.
1933	Konstantin Päts, prime minister since independence, appoints himself dictator after the failure of a right-wing coup attempt.
1940	Following the Molotov-Ribbentrop Pact between Nazi Germany and the USSR, Estonia is invaded by the Red Army and forcibly merged with the USSR, becoming a Soviet republic. Tens of thousands of Estonians suspected of opposing the Soviet regime are killed, deported to Siberian prison camps, or flee the country.
1941–44	Nazi Germany invades Estonia, merging it with Latvia, Lithuania and Belarus into an occupied territory known as Ostland. Around 5,000 Estonian Jews are murdered by the Nazis and Estonian collaborators; up to 50,000 Estonians are enlisted into the Wehrmacht (German Army) or auxiliary units.
1945	Reoccupied by USSR. Up to 70,000 Estonians flee west, following the retreating Germans.
1945–91	Estonia remains under Soviet domination until the collapse of the USSR in 1991. Up to 60,000 people are killed or deported to the USSR's 'Gulag Archipelago' of prison camps between 1945 and 1949. Some escape to the forests, but most are hunted down by the early 1950s. Large numbers of Russians migrate to Estonian towns during the Soviet era, partly to fulfil a need for labour and partly as a deliberate Soviet policy aimed at undermining Estonia's national identity. Tallinn, with a pre-war population of just 175,000, almost doubles in size, mainly due to Russian immigration. Most of Estonia remains off-limits to western visitors throughout this period and the country's coasts are heavily militarised. Tallinn, however, becomes a popular destination for visitors from nearby neutral Finland, who are attracted by the low price of alcohol and other goods.

1988 With the Soviet Union becoming less repressive, Estonians are emboldened to seek a greater say in their own affairs. Peaceful protests against Soviet rule and calls for self-government begin in the 'Singing Revolution', with hundreds of thousands of Estonians gathering to sing officially prohibited nationalist anthems. Similar protests take place in the other Baltic Soviet republics. Estonia's ruling council, the Supreme Soviet, declares national sovereignty within the USSR.

1991 National referendum returns huge vote in favour of splitting from USSR. Full independence is declared on 20 August.

1992 Estonia officially adopts a new, democratic constitution. The country's first freely contested general election is won by the centre-right Fatherland party.

1995 Last Russian garrisons withdraw from former Soviet bases in Estonia.

1996 An agreement between post-Soviet Russia and Estonia is initialled, formally recognising Estonian independence. Estonia renounces claims to border territory east of the River Narva. Stumbling blocks included Estonia's tardiness in granting full citizenship to all its Russian-speaking residents.

2004 Estonia joins the European Union (EU) and NATO, opening up the economy to greater investment from western Europe.

2006 Toomas Hendrik becomes president.

2007 Reform Party wins parliamentary elections. Removal of Soviet war memorial in Tallinn provokes violent protests by ethnic Russians.

Politics

Estonia's history has given it little preparation for good governance, but the country has managed its transition from the one-party state of the Soviet era to true multi-party democracy with remarkable ease and a notable absence of violence, even during the tense period of the collapse of the USSR and the withdrawal of Red Army troops from their Estonian bases.

Until the arrival of the crusader Knights of the Sword in the 13th century, Estonia seems to have been a loose federation of clans and tribes which coexisted in relative harmony.

Baltic barons

The Middle Ages saw the imposition of the hegemony of German nobles, bishops and archbishops, who controlled vast land holdings and serfs who were slaves in all but name.

While the country changed hands between the great powers of northern Europe, these aristocrats remained in control until the 20th century, when the Estonian people first began to demand more freedom.

War and revolution

The Baltic German barons met their nemesis with World War I and the Russian Revolution, which gave Estonia its first brief taste of national freedom. Independence, however, did not bring democracy, with Estonia, like its Baltic neighbours, falling under the sway of a 'strong-man' dictator, Konstantin Päts, and the suspension of democratic government.

The Soviet era

None of this gave Estonia much schooling in multi-party governance, while the sham-democracy of the Estonian Soviet Republic from 1945 to 1991 proved no better – so it is a credit to the instincts and courage of the Estonian people that they have taken so little time to create, virtually from scratch, a functioning democratic nation.

Modern politics

That said, the young republic has had its teething problems. Relations between Estonia and Russia remain chilly, but Estonia's entry into the EU and NATO has given it powerful allies and greater confidence in dealing with its big neighbour to the east.

The constitution, which was adopted in 1992, provides for a single-chamber,

101-seat parliament, the Riigikogu, members of which are elected every four years.

The president is the head of state and is elected for a five-year term. The president appoints a prime minister with the approval of a majority of members of parliament. The prime minister in turn selects a Council of Ministers, who must also be approved by parliament. Presidential elections were last held in 2006; Parliamentary elections were last held in 2007.

Estonia's first democratically elected president was the author Lennart Meri, who had been foreign minister of the republic during the Soviet era. Meri was elected for a second term in 1996. Toomas Hendrik Ilves, the current president, was elected in 2006.

Political parties

Since independence, Estonia has been a multi-party democracy with a vengeance, and no single party has been able to command an unchallenged majority in parliament.

Parliament has 101 seats and is dominated by two main parties, the Centre Party and the Reform Party. The latter won the 2007 parliamentary elections with 31 seats, and formed a governing coalition with the smaller Union of Pro Patria and Res Publika (IRL), which won 19 seats. The Centre Party won 29 seats. Smaller parties include the Social Democrats with ten seats in 2007, the Greens with six seats, and the Estonian People's Union, also with six seats.

The Estonian national flag and European Union (EU) flag

Since independence, no single party has emerged with a truly commanding majority in parliament, and ideological differences between parties are narrow. Most espouse a centre-right, free-market stance and have enthusiastically embraced membership of the European Union and greater monetary and political integration within the EU. The ethnic Estonian majority feels no nostalgia for the Soviet era, and symbols such as the hammer and sickle, statues of Soviet leaders and even Soviet war memorials have been relegated to museums and antique shops. The country's Russian minority, however, feels close ties to its compatriots across the border. In 2007, the removal of the massive war memorial statue of a Red Army soldier from its site in central Tallinn triggered violent protests from ethnic Russians. In Russia itself, the Estonian embassy was attacked by rioters, the Russian government made its displeasure clear, and Estonia's web infrastructure suffered what appeared to be a well-coordinated 'cyber-war' attack from ethnic Russian sympathisers.

In such a small country, there is little cause for conflict between central government and regions, but for administrative purposes Estonia is divided into 15 counties or maakonnad: Harjumaa, Hiiumaa, Ida-Virumaa, Järvamaa, Jögevamaa, Läänemaa, Lääne-Virumaa, Pärnumaa, Põlvamaa, Raplamaa, Saaremaa, Tartumaa, Valgamaa (Valga), Viljandimaa and Võrumaa.

Agriculture is still vital to the economy

The economy

Even under Soviet rule, Estonia was relatively prosperous, thanks mainly to trade with its neutral neighbour Finland, which enjoyed a special economic and political relationship with the USSR. Since independence, Estonia has become one of the more economically successful post-Soviet states, with an enviable growth rate (GDP is growing at six per cent), low unemployment and low inflation.

As a new member of the World Trade Organization and the European Union, Estonia has made an efficient transition to a modern market economy, including the pegging of its currency, the kroon, to the euro. The economy benefits from strong electronics and telecommunications sectors and is greatly influenced by developments in Finland, Sweden and Germany, three major trading partners.

Heavy industry, which played a major part in the economy during the Soviet period, now takes second place to the service sector, which accounts for around 75 per cent of economic activity and employs around 70 per cent of the workforce. Industrial sectors include engineering and electronics, information technology, telecommunications and wood products, accounting for around 28 per cent of the economy, while agriculture accounts for just over 4 per cent. Membership of the European Union offers Estonia challenges as well as opportunities. Inward investment from the EU is likely to increase, but investors will demand a stable economic and political environment and an end to the corruption scandals that have affected virtually every Estonian political party. Estonia is keen to become part of the Euro and Schengen zones, meshing its economy more seamlessly with its EU partners and allowing freer movement of labour and capital, but it must still meet stringent economic and security criteria before it can achieve this goal.

Hansabank's new building in Tartu is a symbol of Estonia's booming wealth

For the visitor, EU membership has already eased the formalities of entering Estonia, and visas are no longer required for citizens of EU member states.

The Hanseatic League

The merchants of Tallinn – then known as Reval – opted to join the Hanseatic League in 1285, a move that made their city part of one of the most remarkable trade networks of medieval Europe. It bought them the protection of a mercantile alliance whose activities ranged south as far as Bruges in Flanders, eastward to Novgorod in Russia, northward to Bergen on the west coast of Norway and westward to London.

The *Hanse* (medieval German for 'guild') was founded by north German merchants and controlled much of the trade of northern Europe from the early 13th century until the late 15th century. Its headquarters was in Lübeck, on the Baltic coast of Germany, but the *Hanse* quickly expanded its Baltic operations to Visby, on the island of Gotland in Sweden.

Visby had been a centre of Baltic trade since the time of the Vikings, and Hanseatic merchants followed long-established trade routes to bring Reval, Dorpat (Tartu) and Pernau (Pärnu) into their commercial network.

Arguably, the *Hanse* was Estonia's first true civilising influence. Its traders built walled towns, harbours, castles and lighthouses to protect their ships and their overland caravans.

From Muscovy (Russia) and the Baltic region, Hanseatic merchants sought raw materials and produce such as furs, amber, timber, pitch (from Estonia's vast pine forests), honey and flax. In exchange, they brought cloth, iron tools and weapons, and other manufactured goods from the more sophisticated economies of Britain and central Europe.

In the 1360s, the *Hanse* showed that it could act forcefully to defend its members' interests, raising an army of mercenary soldiers to defeat the ambitions of King Valdemar IV of Denmark and force him to acknowledge the League's control of virtually the entire Baltic coast.

At its most powerful, during the late 14th century, the *Hanse* comprised an alliance of more than 100 seaports and trading posts, and its regular assemblies or *diets* – which were usually held in Lübeck – aimed to resolve disputes between member cities peacefully. But as the nation states of northern Europe grew larger and stronger during the 15th century, the *Hanse* cities were less able to maintain their alliance. The Novgorod

Merchant houses in the centre of Tartu, a major commercial centre for the Hanseatic League

settlement was closed down by Ivan III, Czar of Muscovy, in 1494. Eastward trade dwindled, and Tartu lost its importance as a staging post. Meanwhile, Sweden had become the dominant economic and military power in the Baltic, and the long conflict between Swedes and Russians in the second half of the 16th century ruined Baltic trade for decades. By the time the Hanseatic League's last *Diet* met in 1669, Reval and Dorpat had passed into Swedish hands and the *Hanse* had long ceased to be a significant force in Estonian history.

Culture

Estonia's national culture was repressed for centuries by the foreign powers which successively occupied the land, and began to flourish only in the 19th century, when authors and playwrights first began to write extensively in the Estonian language.

Authors and playwrights

The keystone of Estonian literature is the *Kalevipoeg* (*Son of Kalev*), an epic tale of a mythical Estonian hero that echoes the Anglo Saxon *Beowulf* or the English *Morte d'Arthur* – though it is in fact the work of a 19th-century German-Estonian, Friedrich Reinhold Kreutzwald, who composed it between 1857 and 1861. Kreutzwald, in turn, took his inspiration from a Finnish epic poem, the *Kalevala*, which also recounts the rise and fall of a legendary warrior-king.

Golden age

A brief 'golden age' for Estonian literature coincided with the two decades of national independence between 1919 and 1940, when authors such as Anton Hansen Tammsaare (1878–1940) were able to publish their work in Estonian. Tammsaare is best known for his epic novel of village life *Truth and Justice*, and those interested in his literary career should visit the Tammsaare Museum in Tallinn, housed in the author's former home, which is dedicated to his life and works. A contemporary of Tammsaare's was Eduard Vilde (1865–1933), a prolific author whose work was deeply influential on the Estonian literary scene, while the earlier Lydia Kolde (1843–86) helped to inspire, and was inspired by, Estonia's search for a national cultural identity.

Oral traditions

Many of Estonia's writers drew extensively on the nation's rich oral folklore, which undoubtedly helped to keep the national culture alive during the centuries of foreign rule.

More recent authors include Jaan Kross and Arvo Valton, both of whom were for a while exiled to Siberia after their works, published during the Soviet occupation, offended the Soviet censors. Kross, like the poet Jaan Kaplinski, was elected a member of Estonia's first free parliament in 1992, and another leading

Estonian poet, Paul-Erik Reemo, became the new republic's first Minister of Culture in the same year.

Music and song

Like its neighbour Latvia, Estonia has a long tradition of epic songs, ballads and sung poetry that celebrate the seasons, the land, romance, family and legends of national heroes that stretch back in time, before the country's conversion to Christianity.

The oldest style of unaccompanied Estonian music, the runic chant, is believed to date back as far as 1000 BC, and these runic verses with their eight-syllable lines are still extemporised on special occasions such as weddings on the Baltic island of Kihnu, in the Gulf of Rīga.

Statue of F R Kreutzwald, father of Estonian literature, at Tartu

Estonia owes a debt to the 19th-century musician Jacob Hurt for the preservation of thousands of folk songs and tunes, which Hurt painstakingly collected and wrote down for the first time. Estonians are more closely in touch with their traditional musical culture than most other Europeans, and there are regular performances of folk music and poetry throughout the year.

The most impressive of these are the national song festivals which take place every five years and which attract hundreds of thousands of spectators and performers, many of them dressed for the occasion in colourful traditional costume. Festivals like these played a major role in the campaign for independence during the late 1980s, which is now known as the 'Singing Revolution'. The largest such event drew up to 300,000 people in a massive show of peaceful protest and national solidarity. Many traditional songs and chants are unaccompanied, but Estonia also has its own array of musical instruments, notably the *kannel*, a version of the zither.

Open-air music festivals are popular, and include not only traditional music and song but jazz, rock, opera and classical music events.

The country's leading contemporary classical composers include Arvo Pärt, who is regarded as one of Europe's outstanding composers and whose minimalist compositions are clearly influenced by his country's ancient choral vernacular music. Veljo Tormis, another outstanding contemporary musician, is also very strongly influenced by Estonia's unique tradition of runic chants.

Art and architecture

Estonia's outstanding musical tradition is not matched by its achievements in the visual arts. Few outside the country have heard of Kristjan Raud (1865–1943), who is revered in Estonia as the illustrator of the *Kalevipoeg* saga and a leader of the renaissance of Estonian culture. Raud – who worked mainly in woodcuts, developing a distinctive style – was a founder of the 'National Romantic' school, whose followers dealt with many of the same themes as those celebrated in Estonian songs and chants: the seasons, the country and the family. Raud's home in Nomme is preserved as a museum of his work and of prints and paintings by other Estonian artists of the 19th and 20th centuries. Raud continues to influence contemporary artists, including the printmaker Kaljo Põllu, whose work includes a series of prints entitled *Dialogue with Kristjan Raud.*

Most modern Estonian painters – including Raul Meel, Sven Saag and Aili Vint – have opted to work in various abstract forms. Jüri Arrak and Marcus Kasemaa both create fairy-tale images, while Lembit Sarapuu's hallucinogenic, imaginary landscapes show the influence of the Spanish surrealist Salvador Dalí and the Belgian René Magritte.

The visual arts suffered under repressive governments for much of the 20th century, but since independence they have taken on new life. Work by some of the country's most treasured painters and sculptors and by some of the most adventurous of Estonia's contemporary artists can always be seen at the exciting Kumu art museum, at Tallinn's Kadriorg park, and in the city-centre Tallinn Art Hall. The Applied Art Museum, also in Tallinn, regularly displays works by the latest generation of Estonian art students. Guests at the Hotel Pallas in Tartu – built on the site of the country's first art college, which flourished between independence and World War II – stay in rooms individually decorated with copies of works by some of Estonia's leading painters of that era. Pärnu is also a hotbed of contemporary arts. Its Museum of New Art and the Pärnu City Gallery both show work by the new generation, and you can see some of the city's painters, sculptors and printmakers at work in the Pärnu Artists House, where several studios are housed in a pre-World War II mansion.

To give credit to the USSR's cultural *apparatchiks*, they oversaw the restoration of many of the fine historic buildings of Tallinn and other Estonian cities that had been heavily damaged by fighting in World War II. These include buildings such as Lutheran churches built during Swedish rule, town halls, country manors and other official buildings in a distinctive Baltic style that also owe much to Swedish and Germanic architectural traditions, and striking medieval castles.

One of the unusual works of art displayed in the gardens of Sagadi Manor

Festivals

Estonia has a crowded calendar of festivals devoted to music and song, at indoor and outdoor venues throughout the country.

A high point, held every five years (the next one is due in 2009) is the **All Estonia Song Festival**, which attracts an audience of 100,000 or more and culminates with the singing of folk anthems by a choir of as many as 30,000 voices. The **Baltika folk festival**, a feast that rotates between the three Baltic republics, is another important event and is scheduled to be held next in Tallinn in 2009.

The **Tallinn Song Bowl**, a huge open-air arena, is purpose-designed for huge musical events like these, and the Rocca al Mare Open-Air Museum is another favourite outdoor festival venue.

Estonian musical tastes are by no means limited to traditional and classical music – the country has many home-grown rock bands, who get plenty of exposure to enthusiastic fans at several summer open-air rock festivals.

Audience at the All Estonia Song Festival 2004, at Tallinn's Song Bowl. The next Song Festival is scheduled for 2009

March

Setu Lace Day

Traditional folk festival held at Obinitsa, in the Võrumaa region.

Kuressaare Theatre Week

Several days of productions of new and classical Estonian and international drama.

April

Jazzkaar

This is an international Jazz Festival held in Tallinn. This event attracts performers from neighbouring Baltic countries and further afield to venues in the Estonian capital.

May–June

Old Tallinn Days

Festival of music and dance held at various open-air and indoor venues in the old quarter of Tallinn. Starts last weekend in May.

Memme-taadi Festival

This annual folk cultural event takes place in mid-June at Tallinn's Rocca al Mare Open-Air Museum.

Jaanipäev (Midsummer/St John's Day)

Bonfires, fireworks, singing and more organised festivities in all main towns (23–24 June).

July

Beer Summer

Beer, music and dancing at the Song Bowl, first weekend in July.

Vita Saru Folk Festival

Held every two years in the grounds of the Palmse Manor House in Lahemaa National Park, usually at the end of the first week of July. Next due in 2008.

Baltika Annual International Folklore Festival

This week-long event featuring musicians, dancers and costumed parades comes to Tallinn every three years and is next scheduled for the Estonian capital in 2009.

Tallinn Rock Summer

Three days of the loudest, fastest and best in Baltic rock and pop with bands from around the world at Tallinn's Song Bowl.

Viljandi Folk Festival

This event takes place on the third weekend in July, in Viljandi.

August

Classical Music Festival

Performances of new and old classical music by Estonian and international ensembles in Pärnu.

Folk Music Festival

This event takes place every summer, from mid- to late August in Pärnu.

Festival of the White Lady

Estonia's most famous phantom appears at the grand finale of this week of music and dance performances in Haapsalu.

December

Tallinn Winter Week

Music, dance and other events at venues throughout Tallinn Old Town in late December.

Estonian choirs

The roots of Estonia's tradition of choral singing are lost in the mists of time, but the choirs and song festivals that are, even today, part of the Estonian way of life began in the early 19th century. The choirs were mainly formed by schools and Lutheran churches, and led by schoolteachers, ministers and church clerks. Among the earliest were the Torma choir, founded in 1844, and the Põltsamaa choir, formed in 1840.

Much of the credit for making choirs popular in Estonian life must go to Johann Voldemar Jannsen, the Pärnu schoolmaster who founded the Vanemuine Society, the first ever Estonian-language theatre troupe, and launched the first All-Estonian Song Festival in 1869, attracting just 845 singers – a tiny number compared with the 300,000 who turned out to protest in 1991, against Soviet rule, in song, during the 'Singing Revolution' that began in the late 1980s.

Such regional gatherings and festivals soon became an important part of the Estonian national revival, encouraging a wider repertoire and the formation of new kinds of choirs.

Only male-voice choirs took part in the first three national festivals, but mixed choirs were welcomed for the first time at the fourth All-Estonian festival in 1891. However, it was not until 1938 that all-women choirs were allowed to take part, and the first children's choirs participated in 1923.

In 1921, the Union of Estonian Singers was founded to organise song festivals, and promote choral singing and wind-band music. The Union quickly became Estonia's most influential publisher of choral music, organising song competitions and workshops for musicians. Although song festivals and choirs are closely linked with Estonia's struggles for nationhood and independence, they were allowed to continue under Soviet rule, when the first schoolchildren's song festivals were launched in 1962.

From the 1960s, the USSR pursued a policy of encouraging folk music which was seen not only as an important form of authentic proletarian culture but also as a kind of safety valve to allow Estonians (and other Soviet nationalities) to celebrate their distinctive culture without allowing it to become an expression of anti-Soviet nationalism.

Folk ensembles were formed with government approval to perform traditional songs, music and dances, and anthologies of folk music and recordings of folk songs and instrumentals were published.

Meanwhile, thousands of Estonians who were forced to flee their homeland kept the singing tradition alive in exile, as far away as the USA, Canada and

Young choir singers

Australia. Some of them were able to return to take part in the 21st All-Estonian Song Festival in 1991, just as Estonia won independence.

Today, Estonia's marvellous choirs are an inspiration to a new generaton of singers and performers, and flourish as never before. The chance to take part in one of the country's legendary song festivals is an opportunity not to be missed. Visitors to Estonia can find out dates of festivals during their visit from the Estonian Tourist Board, local tourist information offices, or from the listings magazines, *City Paper* and *Tallinn In Your Pocket*.

Impressions

A visit to Estonia does not require lengthy planning or special clothing or equipment. With the expansion of cheap flights from the UK and elsewhere in Europe that can be booked online, Tallinn has become a popular destination for spur-of-the-moment short breaks, with minimum luggage. A winter visit or a longer touring holiday may need just a little more preparation than a short summer break.

When to go

Estonia can be visited all year round, and arguably its picturesque capital looks even more romantic under a blanket of crisp winter snow. That said, most people prefer to visit the country between May and September, when the days are long and the weather can be surprisingly warm and sunny. July and August are the warmest months of the year, with temperatures up to around 23–25°C (73–77°F), but can also be showery. July and August are also good times to experience Estonia's distinctive musical culture, with many of the country's major music festivals taking place during these summer months.

However, as they are also the most popular holiday months for most European travellers, hotels and airlines are busy and prices are higher in summer peak season than at other times of year.

Where to go

Many visitors to Estonia travel no further than Tallinn. The Estonian capital certainly has enough to keep even the most demanding visitor occupied, day and night, for more than a few days, with plenty of museums and sights, a nightlife so lively that it can be exhausting, good shopping and lots of places to eat and drink.

For a taste of the lovely Estonian countryside within easy reach of the capital, travel to Lahemaa National Park, an expanse of more than 650sq km (250sq miles) of coastline, lakes, streams and forests that shelters brown bear, lynx and many smaller mammals, and hundreds of bird species. Further afield, remoter reserves offer even more peace and quiet, with wildlife viewing trips by kayak, canoe or bicycle.

Estonia's lakelands – including the huge Lake Peipsi, scene of an epic medieval battle between Russian and German knights – appeal to those with a taste for natural beauty. Tartu, between Lake Peipsi and Estonia's second largest body of water, Lake Võrtsjärv, is a peaceful university town with the country's finest array of Swedish-influenced neoclassical architecture. It has suffered less than most Baltic cities from the ugliness of Soviet-era construction. It has also, so far, escaped the excesses of western tourism, the more heavy-drinking groups of young British and Irish visitors that flock to Tallinn's bars and clubs.

Estonia's coastline also has plenty to offer, with offshore islands ranging in size from the relatively large Saaremaa and Hiiumaa, off the west coast, to tiny rocky isles inhabited only by a few sea birds. The larger islands, with their beaches and fishing communities, are attractive places for walkers, beachcombers and cyclists in summer, with a smattering of small inns and other places to stay, including wooden cottages for hire. Dozens of tinier, uninhabited islands are dotted across Hullo Bay on the island of Vormsi, while the Matsalu Nature Reserve on the mainland west coast is a haven for huge flocks of water birds.

What to bring

Estonia is a European country with a relatively temperate climate and there is no need to pack an extensive wardrobe, even for a longer holiday.

Few if any restaurants or hotels operate a dress code requiring men to wear a jacket and tie, and there are no restrictions on how women may dress.

A waterproof jacket or coat, hat or umbrella, and a light sweater or fleece are essential even in summer, as rain is common at any time of year.

For visits in winter months, warm footwear that is proof against snow and slush is essential, along with a warm hat, scarf, gloves, sweaters or fleeces and a warm coat or jacket.

Summer is a great time to see the flower-filled meadows on Saaremaa

Street signs help you find your way

Unlike the era of Soviet occupation, when it was advisable to bring even such simple essentials as soap, shampoo, toilet paper and even a bath plug, shops in Tallinn are now well stocked with western toiletries and remedies.

However, visitors who require specific medications or prescription drugs should bring an adequate supply with them.

For summer visits, especially if you are planning to visit the countryside and national parks, bring an effective insect repellent as Estonia's wetlands are a haven for mosquitoes and midges. Repellents with a high percentage of the chemical DEET (diethyltoluamide) are the most effective. Irritating though they may be, there is no evidence that Estonian mosquitoes carry malaria or other diseases.

Bring binoculars for wildlife viewing and birdwatching. Most brands of photographic film for prints are readily available in Tallinn, but not so widely sold outside the capital. Photographers who use professional or specialist film for transparencies, such as Fuji Velvia, should bring an adequate supply as such film can be hard to find.

For those planning a cycling holiday, most airlines will carry bicycles as part of the traveller's checked hold luggage allowance.

Culture shock

Before independence, Tallinn was as grimly intimidating as any city in the Soviet empire. To arrive in Estonia was to step into a world of officious bureaucracy, drably dressed people, omnipresent police and militia, streets crammed with identical, smoke-belching Russian-built vehicles and poorly stocked shops. Hotels and restaurants seemed to take pride in appalling service, shabby rooms and inedible food – and, to western visitors, most of the country was off-limits.

Even in the years soon after independence, visitors were exposed to a certain amount of culture shock. Until Estonia adopted its own currency, the kroon, the Soviet rouble remained officially in use – but at a rate of exchange that made even budget travellers into rouble millionaires, only to find that most bars, hotels and restaurants refused to take the devalued Soviet notes, accepting only hard western currency.

Those days have gone, and Tallinn today looks and feels very much like any other western city, with bright new bars, restaurants serving cuisine from around the world, and shops stocked with western goods that 20 years ago were not available even on the black market.

If there is a risk of culture shock in Tallinn, now, it is in encountering the familiar in an unexpected setting – such as the incongruously large number of Irish-themed pubs dotted around the city centre. That said, Estonia can still serve up a portion of surprises. Not far from the bustling, westernised streets of the city centre lie virtual ghettoes of drab Soviet-era apartment blocks, and Tallinn's apparent prosperity belies the economic hardship that has struck many former workers in its now defunct factories and shipyards – many of them ethnic Russians. Other cities around the country, such as Narva, bear the scars of the post-independence industrial collapse and have still to recover from it. There is still a strong resentment of Russia and the Russians among ethnic Estonians, and an equally strong (though less frequently heard) resentment of the new regime among older ethnic Russians.

Tourists trying to decide where to go next

Enjoying a summer day out on the street

Manners and customs

Like their Scandinavian neighbours north and west of the Baltic Sea, Estonians are so reserved and polite that their calmness and courtesy can seem somewhat aloof, even rude, to people from more excitable nations. This national reserve may be partly due to Estonia's many centuries under the heel of foreign powers, when outspoken frankness and shows of emotion were – to say the least – often inadvisable. Even now, however, Estonians seem reluctant to open up to strangers and even to each other, and it sometimes seems almost impossible to force a smile from waiters, hotel receptionists or store staff. Even so, the modern Estonian service mentality is a million miles from the era of 'unobtrusive Soviet service', when virtually any request seemed to meet the answer 'no'. In general, Estonians are only too happy to help the visitor. Since independence, Estonian business has also acquired a reputation for efficiency and straight dealing that puts the country head and shoulders above many ex-Soviet republics and satellite states.

One habit that seems to indicate their warmer, more outgoing side is the custom of giving flowers – not just on special occasions, but whenever visiting the home of a friend or acquaintance. There is at least one flower market in every Estonian town, flower stalls command many street corners and flower vendors patrol railway stations and bus stops until late into the evening.

Greetings

In keeping with their reputation for reserve, Estonians tend to eschew physical contact, even when greeting all but the closest family members. Shaking hands on introduction is the standard greeting for both men and women, and it is also normal to shake hands on departure. It is also considered courteous for men to rise when a woman enters the room.

Estonians are aware that their language is little understood by visitors and is almost unknown outside Estonia, and show no resentment of this. Many younger Estonians – indeed, virtually all of those working in tourism and related service industries – speak good English and often German as well. The visitor's fumbling attempts to communicate in Estonian are unlikely to attract either praise or criticism. Russian is still very much identified with the Soviet period, and few Estonian-speakers willingly use it, while older Russian-speakers resent being pressured to speak Estonian.

The Old Town square is the meeting point for local Estonians

Tallinn

Straddling an isthmus between the Baltic Sea and Lake Ulemiste on Estonia's north coast, Estonia's capital faces north across a broad bay which offers a natural anchorage and has been an important seaport since early medieval times. With a population of 392,306 in 2004, Tallinn is home to one in three of the country's people, but it is a compact city with an area of just under 158sq km (61sq miles).

The old centre of the city is overlooked by Toompea Hill, crowned by an array of historic buildings spanning more than five centuries. The streets below comprise the most remarkable collections of medieval buildings in Europe. Battlements, bastions, church spires and cobbled, hilly streets dominate the Old Town, which is surrounded by a ring of sturdy medieval walls.

Listed as a UNESCO World Heritage Site since 1997, the old quarter is divided into two parts. The Lower Town, around Raekoja plats (Town Hall Square), is a mixture of old and new, with gracious late medieval buildings surrounding the square and the 14th-century town hall. Overlooking this is the Upper Town, with the towers of Toompea Castle overlooking the whole city.

West of Toompea is a crescent of parks and gardens, while further out from the city centre, the picturesque architecture of the Old Town gives way to an outer ring of drab apartment blocks, factories and docklands. East of the centre lies Kadriorg Park, laid out around a baroque palace built for the 18th-century Russian czar Peter the Great. About a kilometre to the north of Kadriorg is Pirita, Tallinn's water-sports suburb, with its beach, sailing centre and boats for hire.

TOOMPEA HILL (UPPER TOWN)

Tallinn's most picturesque buildings are at the summit of Toompea Hill, looking out over the Lower Town, Tallinn Bay and the modern parts of the city. The old cobbled street called Pikk jalg ('Long Leg') ascends to the top from the 14th-century Pikk jalg gate-tower, about 50m (55yds) northwest of Raekoja plats. From viewpoints along the way, and from Lossi plats at the summit of Toompea, there are striking views of the squares, streets and church spires of the old quarter below – as well as less postcard-pretty vistas of the cranes and docks of the waterfront

Tallinn

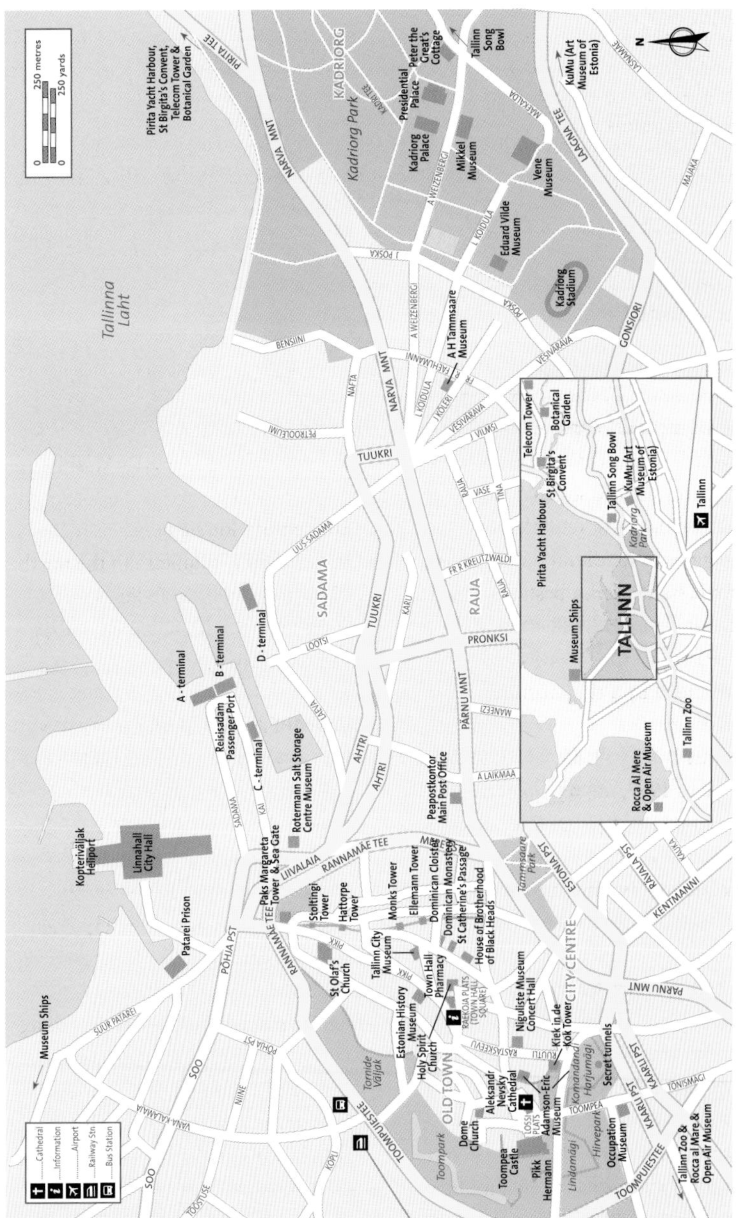

Cathedral
Information
Airport
Railway Stn
Bus Station
0 250 metres
0 250 yards
N
Tallinna Laht
Pirita Yacht Harbour, St Birgita's Convent, Telecom Tower & Botanical Garden
PIRITA TEE
NARVA MNT
KADRIORG
Kadriorg Park
Presidential Palace
Peter the Great's Cottage
Tallinn Song Bowl
KuMu (Art Museum of Estonia)
Kadriorg Palace
Mikkel Museum
Vene Museum
Eduard Vilde Museum
Kadriorg Stadium
LAAGNA TEE
MAJAKA
A WEIZENBERGI
L KOIDULA
J POSKA
MÄEKALDA
GONSIORI
VESIVÄRAVA
A H Tammsaare Museum
BENSIINI
NAFTA
FAEHLMANNI
J KOLERI
J VILMSI
PETROOLEUMI
TUUKRI
RAUA
VASE
TIINA
UUS-SADAMA
SADAMA
FR R KREUTZWALDI
KARU
PRONKSI
LOOTSI
D - terminal
A - terminal
B - terminal
Reisisadam Passenger Port
C - terminal
Rotermann Salt Storage Centre Museum
LAEVA
AHTRI
PÄRNU MNT
MANEEZI
A LAIKMAA
Peapostkontor Main Post Office
KAI
Kopteriväljak Heliport
Linnahall City Hall
Paks Margareta Tower & Sea Gate
LIIVALAIA
RANNAMÄE TEE
Stoltingi Tower
Hattorpe Tower
Monks Tower
Ellemann Tower
Dominican Cloister
Dominican Monastery
St Catherine's Passage
House of Brotherhood of Black Heads
Tammsaare Park
ESTONIA PST
RAVALA PST
KENTMANNI
KAUKA
Patarei Prison
PÕHJA PST
PIKK
St Olaf's Church
Tallinn City Museum
Town Hall Pharmacy
RAEKOJA PLATS (TOWN HALL SQUARE)
Niguliste Museum Concert Hall
CITY CENTRE
PÄRNU MNT
Museum Ships
SUUR PATAREI
Estonian History Museum
Holy Spirit Church
RASTASKEEVU
RUUTLI
Kiek in de Kök Tower
SOO
NIINE
Tornide Väljak
OLD TOWN
Aleksandr Nevsky Cathedral
Adamson-Eric Museum
Komandandi Harjumägi
Secret tunnels
KAARLI PST
TÕNISMÄGI
VANA-KALAMAJA
TOOMPUIESTEE
KOPLI
Dome Church
LOSSI PLATS
TOOMPEA
Toompea Castle
Toompark
Pikk Hermann
Lindamägi
Hirvepark
Occupation Museum
TÖÖSTUSE
Tallinn Zoo & Rocca al Mare & Open Air Museum
Telecom Tower
Botanical Garden
St Birgita's Convent
Pirita Yacht Harbour
Tallinn Song Bowl
Kadriorg Park
TALLINN
Tallinn
Tallinn Zoo
Rocca Al Mere & Open Air Museum

The onion domes of the Aleksandr Nevsky Cathedral

area. The streets and lanes around Toompea attract crowds of visitors, expecially in summer, and are crammed with craft shops, art galleries, souvenir stalls, bars and cafés.

Aleksandr Nevsky Cathedral

With its onion-shaped domes and colourful façade, Toompea's biggest landmark is at odds with the prevailing baroque style of Tallinn's Lutheran churches. This Russian Orthodox cathedral is named after the conquering prince who defeated the Teutonic Knights in the early 13th century. It was commissioned by Czar Alexander III in 1894. Designed by the Russian architect Mikhail Preobrazhensky, it was consecrated in 1900.
Lossi plats 10. Tel: (372) 644 3484. Open: 8am–7pm. Admission free.

Dome Church (Toomkirik)

Tallinn's oldest church is also called St Mary's Church and was built by the first Christian Danes to settle on Toompea in 1219. The existing building is substantially more recent, with a gothic façade that dates from the 14th century and an interior that was rebuilt after being damaged by fire in 1684. A baroque pulpit was added in 1686 and an organ loft in 1780.
Toomkooli 6. Tel: (372) 644 4140. www.eelk.ee. Open: Tue–Sun 9am–4pm. Admission free. Visitors are asked not to visit during services, which are held in Estonian, Sun 10am, and in Latvian every third Sun at 1pm.

Occupation Museum

To understand how most Estonians feel about the period of Soviet (and, briefly,

German) occupation of their country, a visit to this small museum is a must. Focusing on the period 1939 to 1991, the exhibition is far from objective, but it reveals in painful detail the injustices done to the Estonian people during World War II and the Cold War which ended with the collaspe of the Soviet Union and Estonian independence.

Toompea 8. Tel: (372) 668 0250. www.okupatsioon.ee. Open: Tue–Sun 11am–6pm.

Secret tunnels

Originally built to connect the massive bastions built by the Swedes in the 17th and 18th centuries, these spooky tunnels were disused for decades. A stretch of several hundred metres reopened as a visitor attraction in 2007.

Harju Hill. Tel: (372) 644 6646. Admission charge. Advance booking required. Admission with guided tour only: meet at Kiek in de Kok, Komandandi 2 (see p51). Tours leave hourly Tue–Fri and Sun, 11am–4pm.

Toompea Castle

Before the arival of the Danes in 1219, a wooden castle stood atop Toompea. The Danish conquerors replaced it with a stone fortress, which was rebuilt and expanded by successive rulers of Estonia over a period of seven centuries, and which is now the seat of Estonia's parliament, the Riigikogu. Three corner towers date from the days of the Knights of the Sword, who added

Soviet-era statues in the Occupation Museum

Toompea Castle

them during the 13th century. A fourth tower, Pikk Hermann, built in 1371, holds aloft Estonia's national blue, black and white flag. Less forbidding than the original medieval towers is the pink-stuccoed baroque main section, added during the 18th century when the Russian Czarina Catherine the Great had the castle rebuilt in a less militant style. *Lossi plats 1. Tel: (372) 631 6331. www.riigikogu.ee. Admission with guided tour only.*

LOWER TOWN

Town Hall Square (Raekoja plats) is the epicentre of the lower quarter of the Old Town, within the ring of battlements built to defend it against medieval marauders. Once used for open-air markets and public executions, the cobbled square lies to the east of Toompea, with the long, steep street called Pikk jalg leading up to the castle. In the streets around Raekoja plats stand some of the Baltic region's finest examples of baroque architecture, within a ring of dramatic fortifications. This part of town has also become the most stylish shopping area in Tallinn, with numerous designer stores and art galleries. The only sensible way to explore this compact historic centre is on foot.

West of Toompea, a crescent of parks and gardens stretches around the battlements. In summer, the **Komandandi Garden** and the larger **Hirvepark** and the **Toompark** with its landscaped lake are pleasant places for a stroll or a picnic.

Adamson-Eric Museum

This interesting collection features the work of one of Estonia's leading 20th-century artists, Adamson-Eric (1902–68) whose work ranged from painting in oils to furniture and interior design. The exhibition includes his powerful and colour-filled paintings, ceramics, jewellery and other items.

Lühike jalg 3. Tel: (372) 644 5838. www.ekm.ee/adamson-eric/. Open: Wed–Sun 11am–6pm. Admission charge.

Dominican Monastery

One of the oldest buildings in Tallinn, this monastery was founded by monks of the Dominican Order in 1245 and is now a museum. Passageways adorned with remarkable 15th- and 16th-century carving surround a graceful courtyard. The **Cloister** (Claustrum) of the Dominican Monastery (*separate entrance, see p50*) originally comprised three wings, of which only the east wing survives. It houses sleeping quarters, the library, refectory, the prior's apartments and other rooms which allow a glimpse of monastic life in the Middle Ages.

Monastery: Vene 16. Tel: (372) 644 4606. www.hot.ee/kloostri. Open: 15 May–24 Sept daily 10am–6pm. Admission charge.
Cloister: Muurihave 33.
Tel: (372) 511 2536.
www.mauritanum.edu.ee
Open: 15 May–31 Aug daily 10am–6pm. Admission charge.

Exhibits at the Estonian History Museum will give you a clear picture of Tallinn's history

Niguliste Museum – the deconsecrated church now houses some splendid artworks

Estonian History Museum (Great Guild Hall)

The Great Guild Hall, dating from Tallinn's 15th-century heyday as a great Baltic trading city, is one of the lower town's more impressive historic buildings. The collection within leads the visitor through the city's history, from ancient times until the end of the 18th century.
Pikk 17. Tel: (372) 641 1630. www.eam.ee. Open: Mon–Tue & Thur–Sun 11am–6pm. Admission charge.

Holy Spirit Church

The beautiful bell tower of this graceful 13th-century baroque church is a much-photographed Tallinn landmark. Within, the interior is a treasury of baroque wooden carving, with a Renaissance pulpit that is the oldest in Estonia. The church became a Lutheran place of worship following the Reformation in the 16th century and is still used for services (*in English daily 3pm*). There are also classical music performances (*Mon 6pm*).
Pühavaimu. Tel: (372) 644 1487. Open: Mon–Fri 9.30am–5.30pm, Sat 10am–6.30pm. Admission charge for music performances. Classical music hour Mon 6–7pm. Admission charge.

Niguliste Museum-Concert Hall

Part of the Art Museum of Estonia, this splendid deconsecrated 13th-century church houses paintings including Bernt Notke's 15th-century *Danse Macabre* and other outstanding works of religious art, including baroque and Renaissance chandeliers, 15th- and 16th-century altars, and the famous Silver Room displaying the treasures of the wealthy trade guilds and religious foundations that dominated medieval Tallinn. Rebuilt during the Soviet era, after being levelled during World War II, the church is also used for organ recitals at weekends.
Niguliste 3. Tel: (372) 631 4330. E-mail: niguliste@ekm.ee. Open: Wed–Sun 10am–5pm. Organ recitals: Sat & Sun 4pm. Admission charge.

Rotermann Salt Storage Arts Centre Museum of Estonian Architecture

This grand warehouse building close to the waterfront (just outside the medieval walls) is one of the most impressive structures in Tallinn's docklands area, where some 19th- and 20th-century industrial buildings are being restored and given a new lease of life. Built in 1908, it was restored and converted in the mid-1990s and now houses a permanent exhibition dedicated to Estonian architecture through the ages and is also used for a changing schedule of exhibitions and other events.

Ahtri 2. Tel: (372) 625 7000. www.arhitektuurimuuseum.ee. Open: Wed–Fri noon–8pm, Sat–Sun 11am–6pm. Admission charge.

St Olaf's Church

Named after Norwegian King Olaf Havaldsson (who was canonised for his role in converting northern Scandinavia to Christianity), St Olaf's was built in 1267 but its interior dates from the mid-19th century. Its 124m (407ft) spire was once (but no longer) the tallest building in Estonia, and it is still one of Tallinn's more prominent landmarks.

Pikk 48. Tel: (372) 641 2241. www.oleviste.ee. Open: 10am–2pm. Services (in Estonian): Sun 10am & 5pm, Mon 5.30pm, Thur 6.30pm, Fri 6pm. Admission free.

Tallinn City Museum

The core collection of the Tallinn City Museum includes everything from medieval weapons, charts and documents to 18th-century household utensils. The museum also serves as a venue for a range of temporary historical exhibitions. The collection is housed in a fine 14th-century medieval merchant's mansion, and the building itself is worth seeing.

Vene 17. Tel: (372) 644 6553. www.linnamuuseum.ee. Open: Wed–Mon 10.30am–6pm. Admission charge.

A view of Tallinn from Toompea

Tallinn city walls and towers

Only about 2km (1 mile) of Tallinn's original fortifications, along with 20 of the 46 towers that once stood at intervals along the battlements, have survived, but the old town fortifications are nevertheless truly impressive. The three oldest towers – the Nunnetorn, Saunatorn and Kuldjalatorn – are open to the public, while two more – **Paks Margareta** and **Kiek in de Kok** – have been turned into museums and the Neitsitorn has become a café with great views. Paks Margareta (Fat Margaret) is a massive 16th-century bastion with walls up to 4m (13ft) thick. It was built to guard the Great Sea Gate which led to the medieval harbour. It now houses the **Tallinn Maritime Museum**, with a collection of model ships, charts and instruments. Outside the museum, a cross stands in memory of those drowned in the sinking of the ferry *Estonia* in 1994. The Kiek in de Kok, which was built in 1475, has an eclectic collection of medieval weapons, old maps of the city, and panoramic views of the Old Town.

Kiek in de Kok: Komandandi 2. Tel: (372) 644 6686. www.linnamuuseum.ee. Open: Tue–Sun 10.30am–6pm. Admission charge.

Tallinn Maritime Museum: Paks Margareta. Tel: (372) 641 1408. www.meremuuseum.ee. Open: Wed–Sun 10am–6pm, closed: Mon–Tue. Admission charge.

Town Hall

The Town Hall or Raekoda is the most outstanding building in the lower town. A stylish Gothic buidling, it was built in 1404 on the site of an earlier building erected in the 14th century. 'Old Thomas', the weather vane which is the symbol of old Tallinn, was added in 1530. Within are vaulted chambers and carved friezes, but the building is still in official use and viewing of the interior is by appointment only.

Raekoja plats 1. Tel: (372) 645 7900. Open: by appointment Mon–Fri 10am–noon & 1–5pm. Admission charge.

OUTER TALLINN

North and east of the city centre – easily reached by tram or bus – are some of Tallinn's most attractive suburbs. Kadriorg, laid out for Czar Peter the Great after he conquered Estonia in the Great Northern War, has leafy parks and an array of museums dedicated to Estonian art and literature.

Kadriorg Palace

Peter the Great ordered the building of this palace for his wife Catherine in 1718, commissioning the Italian architect Nicolo Michetti to design the palace and lay out its grounds, which today are shaded by chestnuts, oaks, linden and lilac trees. During Estonia's first brief spell of independence, it became the residence of the president of the Estonian republic. It now houses

The beautiful Kadriorg Palace

the Estonian Foreign Art Museum. The palace with its three wings is Estonia's only example of northern baroque style, which was also employed in the Czar's palaces in and around St Petersburg. Most rooms are unadorned, providing a plain background for the many exhibits, but the two-storey main salon is dazzlingly ornate.

Peter himself preferred to spend his time in the small wooden cottage behind the Palace, where he indulged his hobby of bootmaking. This cottage now houses the Peter the Great Home Museum, a collection of the Czar's clothes and possessions.

Tram 3. Weizenbergi 37.
Tel: (372) 606 6400. www.ekm.ee.
Open: Wed–Sun 10am–5pm.
Closed: Mon–Tue. Admission charge.

Kadriorg Park

Chestnut trees, lilacs and lindens make this park – originally part of the czar's estates – a very attractive place to wander in summer and autumn.

Tram 3. Off Weizenbergi. No telephone.
Open: daily 24hrs. Admission free.

KuMu (Art Museum of Estonia)

Founded in 1919, immediately after independence, to celebrate and foster the country's visual arts, the Art Museum of Estonia embraces several separate collections in buildings around the capital. The museum moved in 2006 to the new, purpose-built KuMu, a seven-storey museum and gallery complex at Kadriorg, which also houses changing exhibitions of contemporary work by Estonian and international artists.

The Art Museum of Estonia also embraces **Niguliste Museum-Concert Hall** (*see p40*) the **Kadriorg Art Museum**, **Mikkel Museum**, and **Kristjan Raud House Museum**, all in the Kadriorg area.
Weizenbergi 34/Valgel.
Tel: (372) 602 6201.
Open: Wed–Sun 11am–6pm.
Admission charge.

Mikkel Museum

Private collector Johannes Mikkel donated his collection to the Estonian nation in 1994. Now housed in its own building opposite the Kadriorg Palace, it includes sketches by Rembrandt, paintings by other Dutch masters, some superb Russian Orthodox icons and fine ceramics from China and the Far East, reflecting Mikkel's eclectic and exquisite taste.
Tram 3. Weizenbergi 28.
Tel: (372) 601 5844. www.ekm.ee.
Open: Wed–Sun 10am–5pm.
Closed: Mon–Tue. Admission charge.

THE TALLINN CARD

For those planning to make the most of a stay in Estonia's pretty capital, the Tallinn Card is invaluable. This city pass gives free entrance to museums and main attractions in and around the city, sightseeing tours, free city transport and discounts in shops and restaurants. The Tallinn Card is available as a six-hour, 24-hour, 48-hour or 72-hour pass and is sold at the Tallinn ferry terminals, the airport, main hotels and at the Tallinn Tourist Information Centre. Prices start at EEK 90 for a six-hour card, children half price.
Tourist Information Centre: Kullassepa 4/ Niguliste 2. Tel: (372) 645 7777. tallinncard@tallinnlv.ee

Presidential Palace

Built in 1938 as the official residence of the president of the republic, this building echoes the Northern baroque style of the Kadriorg Palace. Used only briefly for its original purpose, it came into its own again after 1991 and is now once again the president's official home. It is not normally open to the public, but the exterior, and the brightly uniformed military guard of honour, are worth a quick look.
Weizenbergi 3. Closed to visitors.

A H Tammsaare Museum

This charming old wooden house was the home of one of Estonia's most important authors. It was here that he wrote his epic five-volume novel, *Truth and Justice.* Visitors without an obsessive interest in Estonian literature will still find that the author's family home, restored and maintained as it was when he lived here in the 1930s, gives an interesting insight into life in Estonia during its brief period of independence before the outbreak of World War II.

Koidula 12a. Tel: (372) 601 3232.
www.vilde.tammsaare.ee.
Open: Mon & Wed–Sun 10am–5pm.
Admission charge.

Eduard Vilde Museum

This pink-painted baroque building was the official residence of the governor of the Kadriorg Palace, and later became the home of one of Estonia's most prolific authors, Eduard Vilde (1865–1933). It is now a museum

Old photograph from the Eduard Vilde Museum

The Estonian Open-Air Museum at Rocca al Mare

dedicated to his life and works. His study and other rooms have been preserved and restored. The building also houses a small art gallery, the Kastellaani Galerii, with displays of works by modern Estonian artists.
Roheline aas 3. Tel: (372) 601 3181. www.vilde.tammsaare.
Open: Mon & Wed–Sun 10am–5pm.
Admission charge.

Estonian Open-Air Museum

This picturesque attraction gathers together more than 70 traditional wooden buildings from Estonian villages and farms. It stands in the grounds of Rocca al Mare, a mansion built by a wealthy Tallinn merchant in the late 19th century. It is the venue for the colourful Memme-taadi festival of folk dancing and music, which is held every year in June.
Rocca al Mare, Vabaohunmuuseumi tee 12. Tel: (372) 654 9100. www.evm.ee.
Open: May–Sept daily 10am–8pm; Oct–Apr daily 10am–5pm.
Closed: 24 June, 24 Dec, 25 Dec, 31 Dec & 1 Jan. Admission charge.

Museum Ships of the Estonian Maritime Museum

Opened in 2005, this is one of Tallinn's newer attractions, with plans to add more ships to the flotilla of historic vessels moored in the city's original seaplane harbour (built in 1916, and historically important in its own right). The collection includes the submarine *Lembit*, which was built in England and was the pride and joy of the independent republic's little navy before World War II, and which served in the Soviet Navy until 1956. Also on display are the mineship *Kalev*, the patrol boat *Grif* and the steam icebreaker *Suur Toll.*
Kuuti 15A. Tel: (372) 641 1408.
Open: daily 10am–6pm.
Admission charge.

Patarei Prison

This gloomy 19th-century fortress on the waterfront was used as a prison between 1919 and 2004, when it opened its cells, work areas and exercise yards to curious visitors.
Suur Patarei. Tel: (372) 504 6536.
Open: Tue–Sat noon–4pm.
Admission charge.

Tallinn Song Bowl

The Tallinn Song Bowl holds a special place in the hearts of Estonians. This natural amphitheatre is the venue for the huge song festivals that are a central part of Estonian traditional culture, which played such a large part in the ousting of Soviet occupiers from Estonia. The Song Bowl normally holds up to 150,000 singers and listeners, but some 300,000 people gathered here in September 1988 to sing national songs in protest against Soviet rule, beginning the 'Singing Revolution' that led to freedom in 1991.
Narva maantee. Open: daily 24hrs.
Tel: (372) 611 2100. Admission free.
Bus 1, 5, 8 or 34 to Lauluväljak.

Two walks: Around the Old Town and Toompea Hill

Tallinn's Old Town is one of the most remarkably intact collections of medieval architecture in Europe, with an array of striking buildings that reflect Tallinn's chequered past. Raekoja plats (Town Hall Square) is the natural starting point for a walk around the historic centre, and above it rises Toompea Hill, with its castle and formidable fortifications. Our walk around the Old Town (orange route) ends at Raekoja plats; to combine it with an undemanding hike to the top of Toompea (yellow route), leave Raekoja plats from the north-west corner, walk less than 100m (110yds) to the end of Voorime, and left on Pikk jalg.

AROUND THE OLD TOWN

Distance: 3km (2 miles).
Time: Maximum 2½ hours for the full walk, depending on how long you stop at each of the sights en route.

The best place to start this walk is at the Paks Margareta (Fat Margaret) tower, at the northern end of Pikk, the Lower Town's main thoroughfare.

1 Paks Margareta

This rugged cannon-tower with walls up to 4m (13ft) thick was built during the 16th century to guard the northern gate which linked the fortified city with its harbour. It now houses the Tallinn Maritime Museum (*see p42*).

From the tower, follow Pikk south – passing between three more medieval bastions, the Fulfordi tower on your right and the Stoltingi and Hattorpe towers on your left – to reach St Olaf's Church, at Pikk 48.

2 St Olaf's Church

This Tallinn landmark was built in 1267, and its original 140m (466ft) steeple made it one of the wonders of the medieval Christian world. In 1820 it caught fire after being struck by lightning and was rebuilt with a more modest 124m (407ft) steeple. The fire also destroyed the building's original lavish interior, and the church was restored in a much plainer style.

From the church, cross to the east side of Pikk. Turn into a small side street, Sulevimägi, which leads almost immediately into Vene, and follow this long street south to the Tallinn City Museum at Vene 17 *(see p41)*.

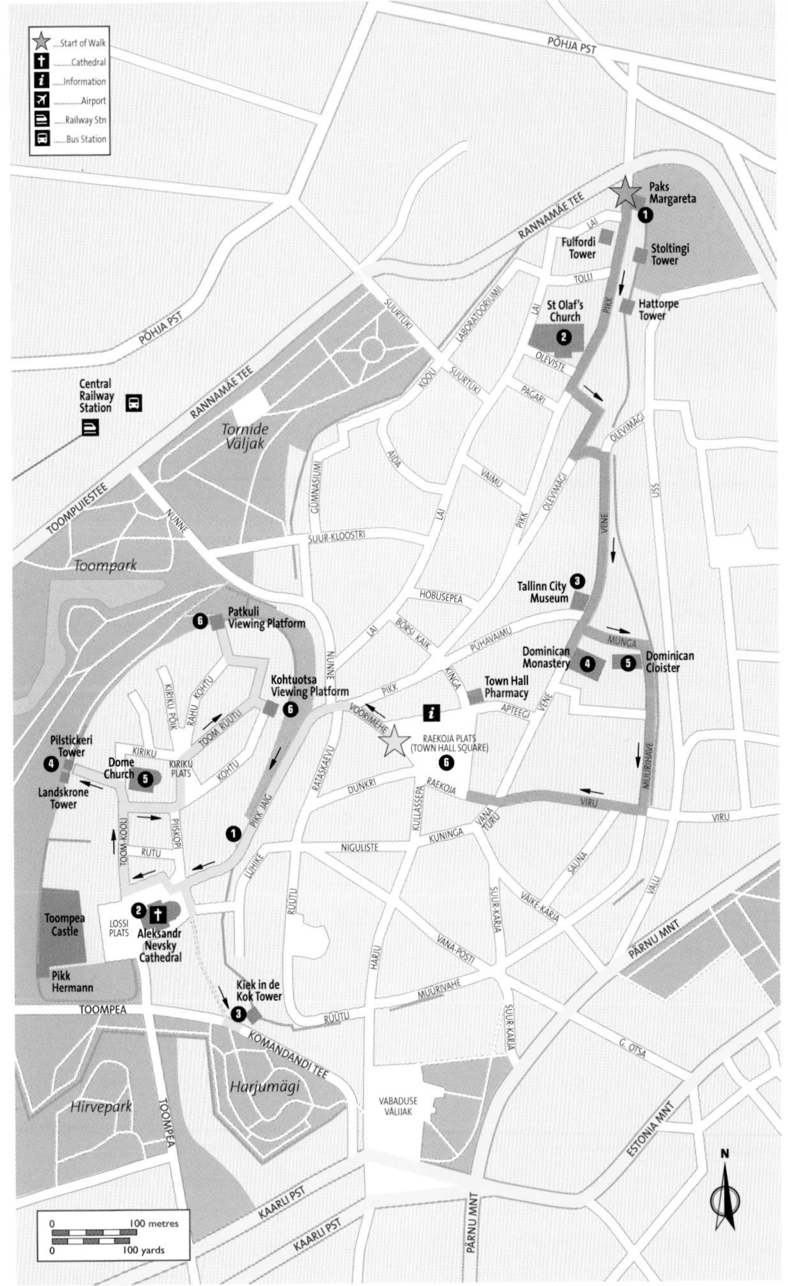
Start of Walk
Cathedral
Information
Airport
Railway Stn
Bus Station
PÕHJA PST
RANNAMÄE TEE
Paks Margareta
Fulfordi Tower
Stoltingi Tower
Hattorpe Tower
St Olaf's Church
Central Railway Station
Tornide Väljak
Toompark
Patkuli Viewing Platform
Kohtuotsa Viewing Platform
Tallinn City Museum
Dominican Monastery
Dominican Cloister
Town Hall Pharmacy
RAEKOJA PLATS (TOWN HALL SQUARE)
Pilstickeri Tower
Dome Church
Landskrone Tower
Toompea Castle
LOSSI PLATS
Aleksandr Nevsky Cathedral
Pikk Hermann
Kiek in de Kok Tower
TOOMPEA
KOMANDANDI TEE
Harjumägi
Hirvepark
VABADUSE VÄLJAK
PÄRNU MNT
ESTONIA MNT
KAARLI PST
G. OTSA
TOOMPUIESTEE
NUNNE
SUUR-KLOOSTRI
LAI
PIKK
VENE
VIRU
MUURIVAHE
HOBUSEPEA
PÜHAVAIMU
MUNGA
APTEEGI
DUNKRI
KULLASSEPA
NIGULISTE
KUNINGA
RÜÜTLI
HARJU
SUUR-KARJA
VÄIKE-KARJA
VANA-POSTI
SAUNA
VALLI
USS
OLEVIMÄGI
OLEVISTE
PAGARI
SUURTÜKI
KOOLI
LABORATOORIUMI
GÜMNAASIUMI
AIDA
VAIMU
TOLLI
BÖRSI KAIK
KINGA
VOORIMEHE
RATASKAEVU
PIKK JALG
LÜHIKE
KIRIKU
KIRIKU PLATS
TOOM-RÜÜTLI
KOHTU
RAHU
KIRIKU PÕIK
TOOM-KOOLI
PIISKOPI
RÜTU
RAEKOJA
VANA TURG
0 100 metres
0 100 yards
N

3 Tallinn City Museum

This 14th-century building was originally the home of one of the city's merchants and was built at a time when Tallinn (or Reval, as it was then known) was one of the wealthiest trading ports in northern Europe. It often hosts quirky temporary themed displays – in 2005 it devoted extensive space to an exhibition of women's underwear from the 19th and 20th centuries.

Continue south for less than one block. The Dominican Monastery is on the east side of the street at Vene 16 (see p39).

4 Dominican Monastery

Although no longer a monastery, this 13th-century religious foundation still exudes an air of tranquillity that makes a change from the tourist bustle of the Lower Town.

Leaving the monastery, walk east one block on Munga, turn south onto Muurihave and find the Cloister (Claustrum) of the Dominican Monastery with its separate entrance at Muurihave 33. The Cloister is open for guided visits only and booking is required (see p39).

5 Dominican Cloister (Claustrum)

Only the east wing of the three cloisters which adjoined the monastery survives, but it is well worth visiting for the insight it offers into the lives of its medieval inhabitants.

Turn right (south) out of the Cloister and follow the road south, parallel to a surviving stretch of the eastern city wall that terminates at the stone towers of the Viru Gates. Here, turn right (west) along Viru, the Lower Town's smartest shopping street, and follow it to its western end; then walk briefly along Vana turu to arrive at Town Hall Square, the very heart of the Lower Town.

6 Town Hall Square

Tallinn's prettiest and most photogenic square is thronged with locals and visitors day and night. On the south side of the square, the Town Hall itself is a stylish, dignified tribute to the city's Baltic architectural heritage. At the northeast corner, the **Town Hall Pharmacy** is a remarkable piece of local history. Built in 1422, it has been in business ever since.

You can combine this itinerary with the Toompea Hill walk; to do so, take Voorimehe from the west side of Town Hall Square to the bottom of Pikk jalg and continue from there (see below).

TOOMPEA HILL

Start this walk at the foot of Pikk jalg, less than 100m (110yds) from Town Hall Square, and allow 3 hours for the entire walk, visiting all the sights en route and stopping once or twice for a drink, a snack, or lunch. In winter, set out around 10am. In summer the sun sets as late as 11pm, so you can enjoy the panorama from the top of Toompea late in the evening, but bear in mind that most museums en route close around 6pm.

Distance: 2.5km (1½ miles).

Time: maximum 90 minutes.

1 Pikk jalg

This steep, narrow, cobbled street links the upper town – the medieval seat of Tallinn's ruling class – with the lower town, where the wealthy merchants made their homes and carried out their trade. It is lined with picturesque old buildings, several with walls that bulge and lean at improbable angles.
Follow Pikk jalg through the lower ramparts to Castle Square.

2 Castle Square (Lossi plats)

Visitors expecting a grim interior to match the forbidding outer aspect of the Toompea ramparts may be surprised by what they find on entering Castle Square. Very little remains of the fortress built in 1229 by the Knights of the Sword, except for the northern and western ramparts, above which rises Pikk Hermann ('Long Hermann'), a 50m (164ft) tower built in 1371. Much less militant is the main part of Toompea Castle, built in the 18th century, which is now the seat of Estonia's parliament. Facing it are the onion-shaped domes of the Aleksandr Nevsky Cathedral, completed in 1900.
From the square, turn downhill towards Komandandi to one of the more quaintly named of Tallinn's surviving medieval towers – Kiek in de Kok.

3 Kiek in de Kok

Its name means 'peek into the kitchen' and this 14th- to 15th-century cannon tower is well named – from its upper windows its garrison could gaze into apartments opposite. It now houses a small museum of arms.
Retrace your steps along the ramparts to Castle Square (Lossi Plats). Crossing the square, walk north on Toom-kooli and turn left towards the twin Pilstickeri and Landskrone towers.

4 Pilstickeri Tower viewpoint

The Pilstickeri and Landskrone towers, along with 'Long Hermann', are the oldest parts of Toompea Castle. From Pilstickeri Tower there are views over Toompea Hill and Toompark.
Walk back to Toom-kooli and the southwest corner of Kiriku Square and the Dome Church.

5 Dome Church (Toomkirik)

Tallinn's oldest church was founded in 1219 and its Gothic façade dates from the 14th century. Within are a baroque pulpit which was added after the interior was damaged by fire in 1686, and an organ loft added in 1780.
From the Cathedral, follow Toom-Rüütli to the north side of the hill, where two platforms afford fantastic city views.

6 Patkuli and Kohtuotsa viewing platforms

Saving the best views for last, stroll along the battlements to the Kohtuotsa viewing platform. Then walk 150m (165yds) north along the ramparts to the Patkuli viewpoint, which offers a fine perspective along the best-preserved northern stretch of the lower ramparts. From Patkuli, steps lead down to Nunne.

Excursions around Tallinn

There is plenty to see within easy reach of Tallinn for those who want to explore beyond the boundaries of the city. Estonia's pretty coasts, offshore islands and national parks are well worth making a short trip away from the city – especially in summer, when long, light evenings allow plenty of time for sightseeing, beachcombing or country walks.

Aegna

Estonia has hundreds of islands (only a few of which are inhabited). Aegna, in Tallinn Bay, is the easiest to visit direct from the capital. This pine-covered island is a perfect place for a family picnic, with tiny beaches, clearly marked walking paths, and forest clearings. Aegna has no attractions to offer the excitement-seeker, but is serene, ideal for relaxing in peaceful surroundings. It is possible to visit for a half-day or a full day, and more self-sufficient explorers can camp overnight.

From Pirita harbour, east of the city centre, ferries leave at 9am, midday and around 6pm in summer; for precise timings check with Tallinn Tourist Information (*Niguliste 2/Kullasepa 4; tel: (372) 645 7777; www.tourism.tallinn.ee*).

Naissaar

Naissaar is larger than Aegna and has a little more to offer the visitor, with very basic hostel accommodation and a modest café in its sole village, Männiku. The island was settled over centuries by ethnic Swedish fisher folk as well as Estonians, but its original communities were ousted by Czarist and Soviet Russian military garrisons in the 19th and 20th centuries. Estonians began to resettle the islands in the mid 1990s and points of interest include the abandoned Red Army barracks and other Soviet military buildings and the deserted ruins of Lõunaküla, which was once the island's main village, but has been deserted since World War II.

Ferries leave daily from Pirita in summer. For timings, check with Tallinn Tourist Information (*Niguliste 2/Kullasepa 4; tel: (372) 645 7777; www.tourism.tallinn.ee*).

Tallinn official sightseeing tour

For those who prefer a guided tour with an expert city guide, or who like the extra comfort of seeing the city from a comfortable coach seat instead

of on foot, the Official Sightseeing Tour combines an escorted bus tour of the main sights of the city with the main attractions of the outer districts of the city, such as Kadriorg, together with a walking tour of the Old Town.
Duration: approx. 3hrs. Reisiexpert, Roosikranti 19. Tel: (372) 610 8616.

Paldiski *(also see p66)*
This half-deserted garrison town and port is an eerie reminder of the grim era of Soviet occupation. The Red Army finally pulled out of Paldiski in 1995 after a 60-year occupation during which ethnic Estonian civilians were barred from living here. Few people have felt any urge to resettle the drab tower blocks abandoned by the Soviet forces, and most of the town's remaining residents are Russian-speakers who opted to stay in Estonia and who face an uncertain future. That said, the opening of a ferry service from Sweden in 2000 offered at least the promise of prosperity and rejuvenation.
40km (25 miles) west of Tallinn. Eight trains daily from Tallinn.

Viinistu Art Museum
This privately owned museum, around 64km (40 miles) from central Tallinn, houses the collection of the Estonian entrepreneur and patron of the arts, Jaan Manitski, who has gathered together some 300 paintings and prints by Estonian artists. The collection spans several centuries, with the emphasis on 19th- and 20th-century and contemporary artists.
Loksa, Viinistu. Tel: (372) 608 6422. Open: Wed–Sun 11am–6pm. Admission charge.

Tallinn Old Town

Saunas

The steamy sauna has been very much a part of the Estonian way of life for centuries, and Estonians indignantly reject any suggestion that sauna is a purely Finnish invention.

Some people claim a spell in the scalding heat is the perfect hangover cure, while others like to take a beer or two into the steam with them. Still others say a regular sauna is essential to good health and a long life.

Taking a sauna is very much a social occasion, when friends and family get together, and the sauna is one of the few occasions when Estonians lose some of their reserve. After all, it is hard to remain cool and aloof when sitting stark naked in a room full of people and a sauna visit is not an occasion to be overcome with modesty.

Wearing a bathing suit is considered unhygienic, but when taking a sauna it is best to take a towel to sit on as the wooden benches can become uncomfortably hot. Public saunas are usually segregated by gender, or have separate hours for men and women, but mixed-sex groups of friends or relatives often share a sauna.

A traditional sauna building

Infrared Sauna at Pirita Top Spa

The sauna's heat is from hot stones that sit on a wood-fired stove or electric hot plate, which is heated to temperatures of up to 100°C (212°F). Small amounts of water are ladled onto the stones at intervals to produce a healthy sweat. Sauna novices should choose the lower benches, which are the least hot. A sauna session usually lasts ten to fifteen minutes. At old fashioned log-cabin saunas, which are still found in camp grounds and country resorts, Estonians traditionally plunge straight from the sauna into the snow or take a dip in a chilly lake. In the city, visitors take a shower to wash off the sweat before plunging into a cooling pool.

A cold drink and a bite to eat are considered essential to complete the sauna ritual.

There are numerous public saunas in Tallinn and in other Estonian towns and cities (*see pp172–5*), and most hotels also have at least one sauna cabin. More old-fashioned establishments include smoke saunas, where visitors relish a combination of wood smoke and steam, while Tallinn's more modern hotels and health clubs offer state-of-the-art infrared saunas in place of the traditional wood stove, but many traditionalists feel that these newfangled devices lack the charm and ambience of the traditional wood-lined cabin.

Tallinn has dozens of saunas, ranging from traditional public steam baths to luxury establishments attached to nightclubs and even restaurants. There is even a floating sauna – and a sauna in a converted fire engine.

Northern Estonia

Estonia's northern coastline is a region of changing natural and man-made landscapes and great historic diversity, bearing the marks of conquerors and settlers, both ancient and modern. There are areas that still show the scars of Soviet heavy industry, alongside regions of untouched natural beauty. Inland, there are lakes and forests, while the coast is lined with dramatic cliffs and shallow bays. This part of Estonia is rich in human heritage, from prehistoric burial grounds to the manor houses of wealthy barons and impressive medieval castles.

For centuries, this was a region where people made their living mostly from the sea, as fisherfolk, shipwrights and seafaring merchants. The long coast, with its many anchorages, also opened the north to influences from across the Baltic, while the region's proximity to Russia also meant that it became

Northern Estonia

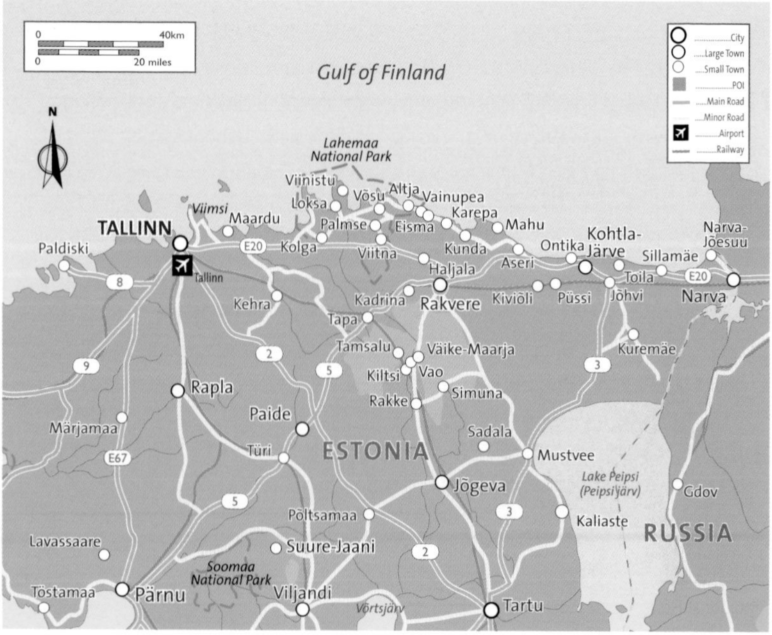

one of the prime areas of Russian cultural and economic influence from the time of Peter the Great until the fall of the USSR.

Soviet occupation spelled the end of a long maritime tradition. With harbours taken over by the Soviet military, Estonians were barred from their own seas, and many fishing communities were wiped out. Some, however, are returning to life, and the grim legacy of Soviet occupation is gradually being reversed.

The north is also easy to explore from Tallinn, even using public transport, as there are frequent trains and buses between the capital and Narva, on the Russian border, stopping at towns and villages en route.

Altja

Altja was a prosperous fishing settlement for more than five centuries until its inhabitants were expelled by the Soviet regime – which, however, began to restore Altja's traditional wooden buildings in 1971, so that the settlement, although still almost deserted, is now a picturesque huddle of homes and boatsheds with a small, old-fashioned inn which was built in the 19th century.

On the coast, 80km (50 miles) east of Tallinn.

Kohtla-Järve

Estonia's fourth-largest city (after Tallinn, Tartu and Narva), Kohtla-Järve is a dour-looking industrial town at the heart of Estonia's oil-shale mining district. It is not the most immediately prepossessing place in Northern Estonia, but its municipality has tried hard to make the most of its industrial heritage. Around the former shale mines, slag heaps – though man-made

Traditional House in Altja

Lahemaa National Park's coastline is dotted with huge boulders

– rank among the highest hills in Estonia; these have been grassed over, landscaped and converted into ski slopes and moto-cross trails, and the town is home to one of the region's more unusual museums, in the western industrial suburb of Kohtla-Nomme. *130km (81 miles) east of Tallinn.*

Kohtla Mine Park-Museum

The region's industrial heritage is celebrated in this unique museum with its tunnels, miniature mine trains, and functioning machinery. Oil shale, a paraffin-rich rock, was widely used as a domestic and industrial fuel until recently, and was a major cause of pollution. Around the former mine, visitors can ski on the landscaped spoil-heaps in winter or rent bicycles in summer, and there is also a 26m (85ft) high artificial climbing wall. *Jaama 1, Kohtla-Nomme. Tel: (372) 332 4017. www.kaevanduspark.ee. Open: Mon–Fri 9am–5pm, Sat–Sun 11am–3pm. Admission charge.*

Lahemaa National Park

The Lahemaa National Park was designated in 1971 to protect the unique landscape of this stretch of forest and coastline. Its name means 'land of bays' and the coastline here is indeed heavily indented, with four rocky headlands separating the large bays of Kolga, Hara, Erü and Käsmu. Huge glacial boulders and sandy beaches such as those at Käsmu and Vösu are typical of Lahemaa's 40km (25-mile) coastline, and inland there are lakes, pine woods and waterfalls. The park has eight well-marked walking and cycling rails, from 1km to 16km (2/3–10 miles) in length, and bicycles can be rented at the park visitor centre at Palmse (*see p60*).

Lahemaa National Park covers more than 700sq km (270sq miles) of almost untouched conifer and deciduous forests, peat bog and sandy coastal plains. Inland, a limestone plateau covered in heath and juniper is bisected by the Estonian Glint, a line of low-lying cliffs that is one of Estonia's major geological features. Within the park, the Viru Raba is a patch of peat bog, covering roughly 3sq km (1sq mile).

More than 10,000 years old, this unique ecosystem is ablaze with colourful wild flowers in spring and early summer.

With such a wide range of environments, the park provides a refuge for a large number of bird, plant and animal species. The most commonly seen are the large mammals, roe deer and elk. There are also large numbers of smaller mammals: hares, pine martens and foxes. Less commonly seen are shy nocturnal mammals such as wild boar and rarer species such as lynx, wolf and brown bear, all present in small numbers. Beaver, though quite common, are not often seen. Lahemaa also harbours some spectacular bird species, including migrant cranes and white storks, which are often seen in the fields in summer. In spring and autumn, lakes and bays are often thick with migrating waterfowl, including grebes and numerous ducks and geese. *Visitor Centre: Palmse Manor, Palmse. Tel: (372) 329 555. Open: daily 9am–7pm. Free admission.*

Käsmu

The pretty village of Käsmu, at the tip of a peninsula that divides two calm bays, made its fortune in the 19th century as a haven for smugglers of salt (which was heavily taxed at the time). It enjoyed a second spell of fortune in the 1920s, smuggling vodka to Finland, where alcohol was banned at that time. Like other coastal towns, it then fell on hard times until independence, but is now becoming a popular spot for wealthy Estonians, who buy and modernise the attractive old shipowners' houses which line its

The Käsmu Maritime Museum

Palmse Manor, one of the most beautiful aristocratic homes

streets. Several of these traditional wooden homes have been turned into cosy bed and breakfast accommodation.

The **Maritime Museum**, housed in the former coastguard station, is a charming private collection of seafaring paraphernalia that has been put together by one Käsmu resident, Arne Vaik.

On the coast, 105km (65 miles) east of Tallinn. Museum: former Coastguard Station, Käsmu. No fax or phone. Open: daily 9am–6pm. Admission free.

Palmse Manor

In the heart of the Lahemaa National Park, this is the most picturesque and striking of Northern Estonia's many aristocratic manor houses. Built for the Baltic-German von der Pahlen family, it was completed in 1740. The owners left in 1923, after their estate was nationalised by the new Estonian government. By 1971 the historic buildings were derelict, but over the next 15 years, they were painstakingly restored and furnished with items similar to those that were owned by the von der Pahlens during the 19th century, including prints and paintings, kitchenware and pretty old-tiled woodstoves. The Manor now houses the Lahemaa Park Visitor Centre, which offers a 17-minute video show in English (*free*) and guided walks in the park. The von der Pahlen family made part of their fortune from distilling vodka, and their distillery has been converted into a comfortable hotel and restaurant.

60km (37 miles) east of Tallinn. Visitor Centre, Palmse. Tel: (372) 329 5530. www.lahemaa.ee. Open: 1 May–31 Aug daily 9am–7pm; 1–30 Sept daily 9am–5pm; 1 Oct–30 Apr Mon–Fri 9am–5pm. Admission free.

Sagadi Manor

Also within the boundaries of the Lahemaa National Park is this carefully restored 18th-century manor house. Once the property of the von Fock family, it is now a hotel managed by Estonia's forestry commission. It also houses a forestry museum, and a collection of amusing modern sculpture adorns its grounds.

Sagadi, Vihula vald, Lääne-Virumaa. Tel: (372) 676 7878. Open: May–Sept daily 10am–6pm. Admission free.

Viinistu

Viinistu, like Käsmu, was a smuggler's village – in fact, it grew so prosperous from running vodka and other liquor to the thirsty Finns that it earned the nickname 'Village of the Spirit Kings'. Although it is less charmingly old-fashioned at first sight than Käsmu, its former fish cannery has been converted into one of the finest collections of works by Estonian artists in the country.

They range from the paintings of Konrad Mägi (1878–1925), Eduard

Sagadi Manor is a beautifully restored 18th-century building

Viiralt (1898–1954) and the early-20th century painter Aleksander Vardi, to experimental work by modern Estonian artists. The museum was founded by the locally born Jan Manetski, who made his fortune managing the pop supergroup Abba after his family migrated to Sweden. He returned to Estonia shortly before the country regained its independence, and launched the museum in 2003.
Loksa commune, 74701 Harju county. Tel: (372) 515 7270. Open: Wed–Sun 11am–6pm. Admission charge.

Vösu

This peaceful little seaside resort has a scattering of places to stay and eat and is a good place from which to explore Lahemaa National Park in depth.
8km (5 miles) north of Palmse.

Narva

Facing across the Narva River, which now forms Estonia's frontier with Russia, Narva is a divided city. Until independence, it formed part of Ivangorod, on the east bank of the river. Now, a tightly restricted border runs between the two cities, and crossing it is a time-consuming process for visitors and residents alike. Narva is heavily industrialised, bearing many of the scars of Soviet-era heavy industry. Most of its people are Russian-speakers, though few seem keen to return to Russia, preferring the relative prosperity of the new Estonia.

Narva was settled in the 13th century and rose to prosperity under Swedish

The huge sandy beach at Vösu is never crowded

rule in the 16th and 17th centuries. The Russian Czar Peter the Great saw its potential as a seaport and expanded its harbour and fortifications, but Narva was very heavily damaged during World War II, and only a handful of historic buildings survive or have been restored. Among the most impressive are the castle, which gazes across the Narva River towards Russia, and the Cathedral of the Resurrection, a striking Russian Orthodox church with elaborate red-brick domes.
180km (112 miles) east of Tallinn.

Narva Castle Museum
Narva Castle, founded in the 13th century by the Danes, is the most spectacular stronghold in Estonia, one of the most outstanding examples of military history in northern Europe. Its ring of ramparts and bastions shows the additions made by successive occupiers of the city, from the original Danish builders to the Swedes who strengthened it as a bastion against Russia, though the Russians ousted them during the 18th century. The museum houses a collection of arms and armour from the medieval period through to World War II.

The castle's tallest tower, the 50m (160ft) high Pikk Hermann, looks across the Narva River to the much more dilapidated battlements of the Ivangorod Fortress, on the Russian side. South of the castle is a riverside park which incorporates the substantial outer bastions which were added to the medieval structure by the Swedes. A copy of the Swedish Lion, a monument built to commemorate the Swedish King Charles XII's victory over the Russians in 1701, stands here.
Peterburi 2, Narva. Tel: (372) 359 9245. www.narvamuseum.ee. Open: daily 10am–6pm. Admission charge.

Narva-Jõesuu
Narva-Jõesuu, at the mouth of the Narva River, was a popular seaside resort for well-off Russians during the 19th century and served privileged Soviet Russians during the 20th century. It still has a certain faded charm; its main attraction is one of Estonia's better beaches, a 13km (8-mile) stretch of sand and pebbles. The beach is now not so crowded, even in high summer, as it is cut off from its former Russian clientele by strict border controls.
10km (6 miles) north of Narva.

Ontika coast
This area of natural beauty forms the highest section of the Baltic Glint, a 1,100km (684-mile) long escarpment that dominates the north Estonian coastline. A 23km (14-mile) stretch of limestone cliffs, rising more than 55m (180ft) above the sea, lies between the villages of Saka and Toila, and a 5.5km (3½-mile) study trail leads to the Valaste waterfall: the water falls 25m (82ft). It is the highest waterfall in Estonia.

Between Ontika and Toila, 115km (71 miles) east of Tallinn. No telephone. Open: daily 24hrs. Admission free.

Pühtitsa Convent

This magnificent complex of Russian Orthodox places of worship was founded in 1891 but completed only in 1910, with the building of the Cathedral of the Dormition. The convent is home to around 80 nuns and novices.

A massive stone wall surrounds the convent, pierced by a rectangular entrance gate and belfry with seven bells, the largest of which weighs 2,648kg (5,838lbs). Visitors can still see the log cabins that once housed the nuns, though most of them now live in more modern brick homes. It is also possible for Orthodox and other Christian visitors to stay in the three simple hostels or the convent guesthouse.

Pühtitsa is Estonian for 'blessed place'. The hill on which the convent stands is believed to have been a sacred pagan site in pre-Christian times. According to the early 16th-century *Syrenets Chronicle*, Pühtitsa was the scene of an apparition of the Virgin, who appeared to a local shepherd as a divine lady standing in an oak grove, with light shining all around her. The shepherd and other villagers searched the grove and found an ancient icon under a huge oak tree. This was the icon of the Dormition of the Mother of God, which is still the main treasure belonging to the convent and which stands, set in a jewelled frame, to the right of the main altar in the **Church of the Dormition**.

With the collapse of the strictly atheist USSR and a resurgence of the Orthodox faith, the nuns (who follow an ascetic, strictly vegetarian way of life) receive thousands of devout Orthodox pilgrims each year. They farm the surrounding land, growing wheat, rye, oats, potatoes, cabbages and fodder for a herd of thirty cows, eight horses, and a flock of sheep. They also have a large poultry farm, hothouses, a bee garden and an orchard.

Their other duties include hay-making, mushroom and berry picking, collecting firewood, planting trees, fishing and cutting ice for cold-storage barns.

Pühtitsa's serene churches and beautiful chapels include the **Church of St Simeon and St Anna**, and the **Church of St Sergius of Radonezh**, both built in 1895. The Church of St Sergius is built on the spot where the Virgin is said to have appeared, known as the Holy Mount, and is noted for its superb, intricately carved iconostasis (icon stand). The church was built in 1895 in honour of the convent's patron, Prince Sergei Shakhovskoy, and houses the Shakhovskoy family sepulchre.

The **Church of St Nicholas and St Arsenius**, built in 1885, pre-dates the foundation of the Convent. Two more recent places of worship, the **Church of St John the Baptist and Isidore of**

The Russian Orthodox Pühtitsa Convent

Tartu, built in 1990, and the **Church of St Alexy and St Barbara**, consecrated in 1986, also merit a visit.

Many of the nuns are talented artisans, embroidering beautiful church vestments, making wooden carvings and painting icons. Their work is on show in the convent's museum.

Kuremäe, 30km (19 miles) south of Kohtla-Järve and 180km (112 miles) east of Tallinn. Tel: (372) 339 2124. www.orthodox.ee. Open: daily 10am–5pm. Admission charge.

Paldiski *(also see p53)*

At the western end of Estonia's northern coast, Paldiski is located on a headland that dominates a sheltered bay. Two offshore islands, Väike-Pakri and Suur Pakri, offer further protection from the elements.

Paldiski's history is closely tied to the decades of Soviet occupation and, before that, to the centuries of Imperial Russian domination of Estonia.

Its fine natural anchorage attracted the attention of Czar Peter the Great soon after his conquest of Estonia at the end of the devastating Great Northern War. In 1715 he ordered the building of a harbour which he intended as the main base for his growing navy. Peter died before the project was completed.

The Russians turned their eyes on Tallinn again in 1939, when it was seized by the Red Navy, and its Estonian residents were expelled. The Soviet armed forces returned at the end of World War II, and for the next 50 years Paldiski was a closed military enclave. Soviet departure in 1995 made Paldiski

Rakvere Castle has seen many occupiers

something of a ghost town, and many if its buildings remain derelict. There are, however, plans to redevelop its harbour facilities for cargo vessels and cross-Baltic ferries.
40km (25 miles) west of Tallinn.

Rakvere

Rakvere is a pleasant provincial town and is a good place for a stopover when touring the sights of the north-coast region. It has a cluster of low-key attractions of its own, including the ruins of a medieval castle, originally built by the Danes and expanded in the 14th century by the knights of the Livonian Order. Rakvere was founded in 1252, and the larger-than-life statue of an auroch (a kind of giant wild ox, now extinct), which roamed the region's forests even as recently as medieval times, was commissioned to mark its 750th anniversary in 2002. With a span of more than 3m (10ft) between its horns, it is the work of the Estonian sculptor Tauno Kangro.
100km (62 miles) east of Tallinn.

Rakvere Castle

Like other Estonian fortresses, the castle has had many occupiers, including Poles, Swedes and Russians, all of whom added various new defences. The castle keep and battlements overlook the town centre. Worth seeing within the castle are a medieval dining hall and a grisly torture museum. Music and dance performances happen here in summer.
Vallimägi, Rakvere. Tel: (372) 507 6183. www.svm.ee. Open: daily 11am–7pm. Admission charge.

Rakvere Citizen's Museum

This interesting little museum is housed in an 18th-century home, and gives a fascinating glimpse into the life of a Rakvere citizen at the beginning of the 20th century. Exhibits include furniture and household equipment, kitchenware, old-fashioned tailor's and cobbler's workshops and a collection of photographs from the 1920s and 1930s.
Pikk 50, Rakvere. Tel: (372) 566 7355. www.svm.ee. Open: Thur–Sat 11am–5pm. Admission charge.

Rakvere Exhibition House

Rakvere's municipal museum has recently been expanded to include exhibits from local archaeological sites and old manor houses, and is well worth a visit.
Tallinna 3, Rakvere. Tel: (372) 507 6183. www.svm.ee. Open: Thur–Sat 10am–5pm. Admission charge.

Sillamäe

Trim and pretty Sillamäe has risen phoenix-like from the ashes of its Soviet past. This seaside town was a favourite resort for the wealthy of St Petersburg in Czarist times – the composer Tchaikovsky was among its visitors. After World War II, however, it became a byword for environmental pollution. One of Estonia's largest oil-shale burning

Interior of Rakvere Citizen's Museum

power plants was built here in the late 1920s. During the Soviet period, it was a centre for uranium mining and processing, and was off-limits to most ordinary Estonians. Major efforts have been made to repair the environmental damage done in those times, and Sillamäe is a remarkably elegant survival. Heavily damaged during the World War II, it was rebuilt during the 1950s as a model Stalinist city for the USSR's worker-elite. Buildings such as the House of Culture are dressed up, with an anachronistic plethora of architectural embellishments. The fake-medieval Town Hall would not look out of place in an American theme park, and the apartment blocks built for Sillamäe's workers boast an array of Soviet symbols.

Almost all of Sillamäe's inhabitants are Russian-speaking, and while few would wish to return to the Soviet era, there is less desire here to remove relics of the USSR. The city museum highlights the dubious achievements of the USSR in its heyday, with displays of Soviet heraldry and technology.
25km (16 miles) west of Narva.

Toila

Estonians still come on pilgrimage to this little coastal village to visit the site of the summer home of Konstantin Päts, the country's much-respected first president. Päts had only five years to enjoy the lavish opulence of his

official residence, which had originally been built by a wealthy Russian entrepreneur. It was purchased by the government in 1935 (shortly after Päts had made himself virtual dictator of Estonia). In 1940 he was deposed and imprisoned by the Soviet invaders, and in 1941 his former home was destroyed as the Red Army withdrew ahead of the advancing Wehrmacht. The entrance gates, terrace and drive are all that remain, but the surroundings – with steep cliffs along the coast to either side and a deep river gorge cutting through the landscaped grounds – are still picturesque.
10km (6 miles) north of Kohtla-Järve.

Väike-Maarja

Väike-Maarja, south of Rakvere, is the most important village in a region which is rich in the medieval and more recent heritage of Estonia's Baltic-German barons and their Soviet successors. Two of the most impressive aristocratic homes, Kiltsi Castle and the Vao Stronghold Tower, present interestingly different aspects of the region's historic architecture from the Middle Ages to the 19th century.
25km (16 miles) south of Rakvere.

Kiltsi Castle Estate

Kiltsi is one of the most striking and original of Estonia's once-grand

Beach at Toila on the Gulf of Finland

The Kiltsi Estate in Väike-Maarja

Baltic-German estates. Founded at the end of the 18th century, it was built on the ruins of a 14th-century medieval stronghold which was destroyed during the Livonian War. Its original owners were the von Gilsen dynasty, but during the 17th and 18th centuries the estate passed into the hands of a succession of aristocratic owners, including the Asserini, the Uexkulls, Zoege von Manteuffel and Rosen families. The present manor house was built for Major Hermann Johann von Benckendorff, who became the owner of the Kiltsi Estate in 1784. The splendid (though rather dilapidated) house is in the early classical style, combining two crescent wings with the old stronghold. The Benckendorff family's coat of arms still decorates the façade of the castle. Later, the house passed into the hands of the von Krusenstern family, and the Admiral's Room, in one of the castle's original round towers, commemorates three generations of von Krusensterns.
6km (4 miles) southwest of Väike-Maarja. Tel: (372) 325 3411. www.v-maarja.ee. Open: Sept–May Mon–Fri 8am–4pm; June–Aug Mon–Tue 8am–2pm, Wed–Fri 8am–6pm, Sat–Sun 11am–7pm. Admission charge.

Väike-Maarja Museum

This museum is one of the few museums in Estonia to focus on the decades of Soviet rule, when it was a successful collective farm. This is a period that Estonia prefers to forget, but the museum sheds fascinating light on a period that now seems both distant and very alien.
Pikk 3, Väike-Maarja.
Tel: (372) 326 1625. www.v-maarja.ee.

Open: 2 May–30 Sept Tue–Sat 10am–5pm; 1 Oct–30 Apr Mon–Fri 10am–5pm. Admission charge.

Vao Stronghold Tower Museum

This medieval tower, built in the 14th century, is one of the very few such strongholds to have survived from the turbulent period when Baltic-German landholders were threatened by uprisings of Estonian peasants. This turbulence culminated in the St George's Eve revolt of 1343, when rebels destroyed many of the wealthy estates of northern Estonia. Perched on a steep hillside, the tower is a square building with four levels, the two lower of which are vaulted. The top floor was the guard tower, while the lower floors were living quarters and storage rooms.
3km (2 miles) southwest of Väike-Maarja. Tel: (372) 326 1625. www.v-maarja.ee. Open: 2 May–31Aug Wed–Sun 11am–6pm. Admission charge.

Viimsi

The Viimsi peninsula, just outside Tallinn, is strongly associated with some of Estonia's most revered political, military and cultural figures, including prime minister Konstantin Päts, the poetess Lydia Koidula, and the author A H Tammsaare. The Metsalkalmistu Forest Cemetery, 2km (1¼ miles) east of the Tallinn seaside suburb of Pirita, is the resting place of these eminent people. General Johan Laidoner (1884–1953), revered as modern Estonia's greatest military leader, lived at Viimsi and his former home is now a museum dedicated to Estonia's military history and the War of Independence.

Laidoner Museum

Estonia's national war museum contains exhibits dedicated to the Estonian armed forces. It also commemorates the career of Johan Laidoner, who rose through the ranks of the Imperial Russian Army, then formed Estonia's first army and led it to victory against the Red Army. Laidoner was deported to Russia after the invasion of 1940, along with thousands of other influential Estonians, and died in prison in 1953.
Bus 1 from Tallinn. Mõisa tee 1, Viimsi. Tel: (372) 621 7410. www.laidoner.ee. Open: Wed–Sat 11am–5pm. Admission free while renovations continue.

ADMIRAL VON KRUSENSTERN

Admiral Adam Johann von Krusenstern (1770–1846), who became the owner of Kiltsi Castle in the early 19th century, was one of Imperial Russia's most famous navigators and scientists, leading the first Russian voyage around the world from 1803–1806 and taking part in many other maritime expeditions. He lived at Kiltsi from 1816–22, while compiling his *Atlas of the South Seas*, the most accurate collection of charts of the Pacific Ocean up to the beginning of the 20th century. He died at Kiltsi in 1846 and was buried at the Tallinn Dome Church by special order of the Russian Czar Nicholas I. The von Krusenstern Fund, launched in 1993, is dedicated to renovating and preserving the castle.

The Imperial legacy

Peter the Great

Estonia's centuries under Russian sway were the outcome of the westernising ambitions of Czar Peter the Great (1672–1725), who became sole ruler of Russia in 1696.

Peter was determined to transform Russia from a backward Slavic realm into a great European power, and the Swedish-ruled Baltic provinces stood in the way of this ambition. Soon after moving his capital from Moscow to St Petersburg, on the Baltic coast, Peter launched the Great Northern War to oust Sweden from its Estonian possessions, and conquered Tallinn in 1710.

Estonians look back on the centuries of Russian rule with little affection, but Peter's enthusiasm for modernisation did bring benefits to the country. Peter introduced the latest technology from Western Europe, did away with the old Russian system of government, and reduced the power of the nobles and the Orthodox church. On the outskirts of Tallinn, at Kadriorg, he ordered the building of a new imperial palace precinct which he visited frequently, though he preferred to spend his time in the small cottage next to the palace.

More importantly for ordinary Estonians, the Russian conquest brought an end to centuries of strife, and Estonia remained untroubled by invaders until the outbreak of World War I in 1914 – the longest period of peace in its modern history. When Peter died in 1725, he left Estonia part of a Russian empire that was far more modern and secure than it had ever been.

Under Peter's successors, the Baltic-German barons remained the most powerful and wealthy class in Estonian society, and several went on to become high-ranking officers in the Imperial armed forces. There was substantial Russian immigration into Estonian cities such as Narva, and the Orthodox church became more powerful – as evidenced by the many grandiose Orthodox cathedrals that were built during the 18th and 19th centuries.

While the 200 or so Baltic-German dynasties prospered, however, the ethnic Estonian population remained subservient, until Czar Alexander I abolished serfdom in the empire in 1816, allowing Estonian peasants to own land. By the end of the 19th century, the Baltic Germans no longer owned almost all the Estonian countryside.

As a Russian Imperial outpost, Tallinn's society aped the manners of the Imperial capital, encouraged by an annual summer influx of St Petersburg's aristocrats. The opening of a railway line between St Petersburg and Tallinn in 1870 made Tallinn one of Imperial Russia's most important industrial seaports, and the Imperial railway also helped to turn Pärnu and Haapsalu into fashionable summer resorts.

On balance, Estonia may have benefited overall from its two centuries as part of Czarist Russia, but the empire blotted its copybook in its final years. In 1905, Imperial troops killed 60 Estonian demonstrators in the streets of Tallinn. Around 500 Estonian nationalists and socialists were executed, and thousands were exiled to Siberia. Czarist Russia's humiliating defeat in World War I and its final collapse in 1917–18 overshadow its few positive achievements in Estonia.

Drive: Lahemaa National Park

This 60km (37-mile) drive starts at Palmse Manor, headquarters of the Lahemaa National Park (around 80km/50 miles from Tallinn) and takes in some of Northern Estonia's most beautiful and varied forest landscapes, coastline, old-fashioned villages and dignified manor houses.

If you are starting from Tallinn, allow 10 hours (a full day) including time for beachcombing, birdwatching and swimming. If from Palmse, you will take about 6–8 hours.

Distance: 60km (37 miles). Time: 6–8 hours.

There are several places along the way for snacks, drinks or meals. *Leave the main north-coast highway (E20) at Viitna (75km/47 miles east of Tallinn) and drive 7.2km (4½ miles) north to Palmse Manor, which is clearly marked by a signpost.*

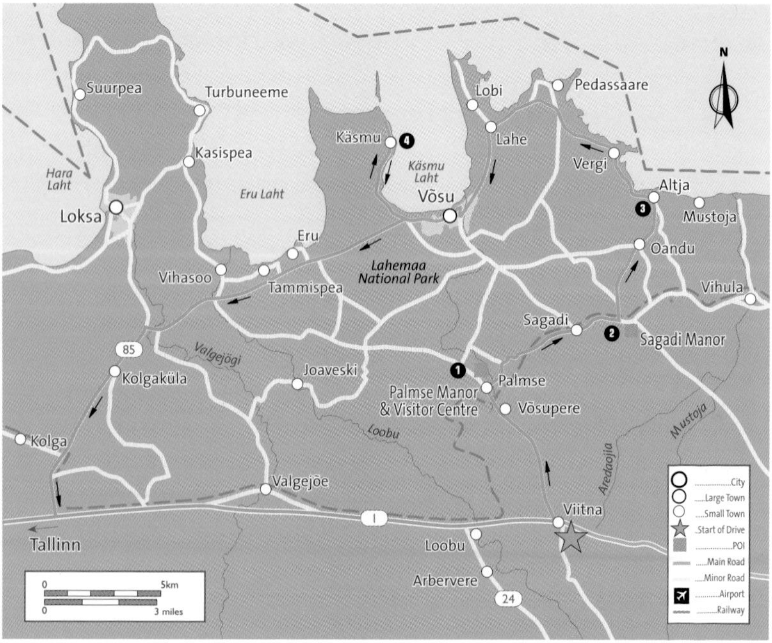

1 Palmse Manor

Palmse Manor was built in 1740; it was the home of the von der Pahlen family until 1923, when the estate was broken up under newly independent Estonia's land reform programme. The manor and its landscaped gardens were restored from 1972 onward. The building now houses the National Park headquarters. Make time to watch the audio-visual programme about the manor and the park, and take a stroll around the ornamental lake. The former vodka distillery, from which the von der Pahlens earned much of their fortune, has been converted into a hotel.
From Palmse, drive 6km (4 miles) eastwards to Sagadi village (clearly signposted) and its manor house, which is 1km (2/3 mile) east of the village, also clearly signposted.

2 Sagadi Manor

Like Palmse, Sagadi Manor was the seat of a wealthy Baltic-German family. The von Focks owned the estate from the early 17th century, but the manor is a mid-18th-century creation, built in the early decades of Imperial Russian rule. Clearly, the von Focks had adjusted easily to life under the Romanov Czars, although they could not match the wealth of their neighbours. Like Palmse, Sagadi eventually passed into the hands of the Estonian state. Restoration of the grounds and building began in the 1970s. The salons and other rooms are furnished with contemporary furniture from the house's heyday.
From Sagadi Manor, take the clearly signposted road to Altja, 8km (5 miles) north of Sagadi.

3 Altja

Still something of a 'ghost town'. It was a prosperous fishing community until the Soviet era, when Estonians were denied access to their own Baltic shores for security reasons. Many of the villagers moved away to seek a livelihood elsewhere. On the positive side, this meant that Altja's charming old wooden buildings escaped demolition or modernisation. Some fishing still continues here. The charmingly ramshackle village inn is a great place to stop for lunch.
From Altja, follow the coast road west for around 18km (11 miles), through the hamlets of Vergi, Pedassaare and Lahe to Võsu, on the curving shore of Käsmu Bay, then head 8km (5 miles) north, still hugging the coastline, to Käsmu.

4 Käsmu

It had a reputation as a smuggler's hideaway during the 19th century, and its wood and brick houses are more substantial than those of Altja. It too languished during the Soviet era, and has the air of a living museum. There is a sandy beach just south of the village – it's a pleasant place for a swim before heading back to Palmse or Tallinn.
For a complete circuit, return to Võsu and turn right. Drive through Kolgaküla to get back to route 1, which will take you left to Viitna or right to Tallinn.

Walk: Around Narva

Narva bears the stamp of Imperial Russian and Soviet hegemony. History's scars are deeper here than anywhere else in Estonia. This walk includes medieval ramparts, 19th-century industrial buildings, a fine Russian Orthodox cathedral and views across the Narva River to the Russian side of the border. There are numerous bars and cafés along the way.

Distance: 3.5km (2¼ miles). Time: 5 hours.

Start this walk at Raekoja plats, in the heart of old Narva.

1 Town Hall

The only landmark of note in the former Old Town (most of which was destroyed during World War II) is the Town Hall. Reconstructed during the Soviet era, building was completed in 1774, the work of the Lübeck master builder, Georg Teuffel.

Leaving the Town Hall, turn west along Rüütli, then take the second turning on your left, along Vestervatti. After about 400m (440yds), turn east (left) at the junction with Peterburi.

2 Narva Castle

Narva Castle was founded in the 13th century, but its most impressive battlements and towers belongs to an age of grim conflict between Sweden and Russia – the Great Northern War, which ended with Russia's conquest of Estonia. Within the castle is a museum, which houses a rather bloodthirsty collection of medieval arms, armour and more recent weaponry. A highlight of the park is the Swedish Lion, a monument to the Swedish King Charles XII's victory over the Russians in 1701.

Climb the 50m (164ft) high Pikk Hermann tower for a view across the Narva River to the Ivangorod Fortress.

From the castle, return to Vestervatti then walk west on Raja and continue to the west end of Malmi. Turn left here and walk south to the Russian Orthodox Cathedral.

3 Narva Cathedral

The Cathedral of the Resurrection is an ungainly yet spectacular collection of red-brick vaults and domes. It was founded in 1890, during the reign of Czar Alexander III.

Walk east along Grafovi, then take the third turning on your right to the

Narva Castle museum *Peterburi 2, Narva. Tel: (372) 359 9230. www.narvamuuseum.ee. Open: Wed–Sun 10am–6pm. Admission charge.*

Lutheran Church of St Alexander (Aleksandrikirik) in its own square.

4 Alexander Church

This Lutheran church was built in 1884 to minister to the workers at the Krenholm factory, which then employed most of the city's workforce. It is currently undergoing restoration.

Turn left, then left again on Kiriku and follow this to the railway station. Cross by the bridge and follow Kalda south for 200m (220yds).

5 Krenholm Works

Three massive brick towers dominate this 19th-century building, which was once the biggest textile mill in Estonia. In the late 19th century, and during the Russian Revolution, the Krenholm Works was a revolutionary hotbed, and under the Soviet regime the factory was regarded as a model of socialist industry. It was privatised after independence.

Tours can be arranged through the Narva tourist information office.

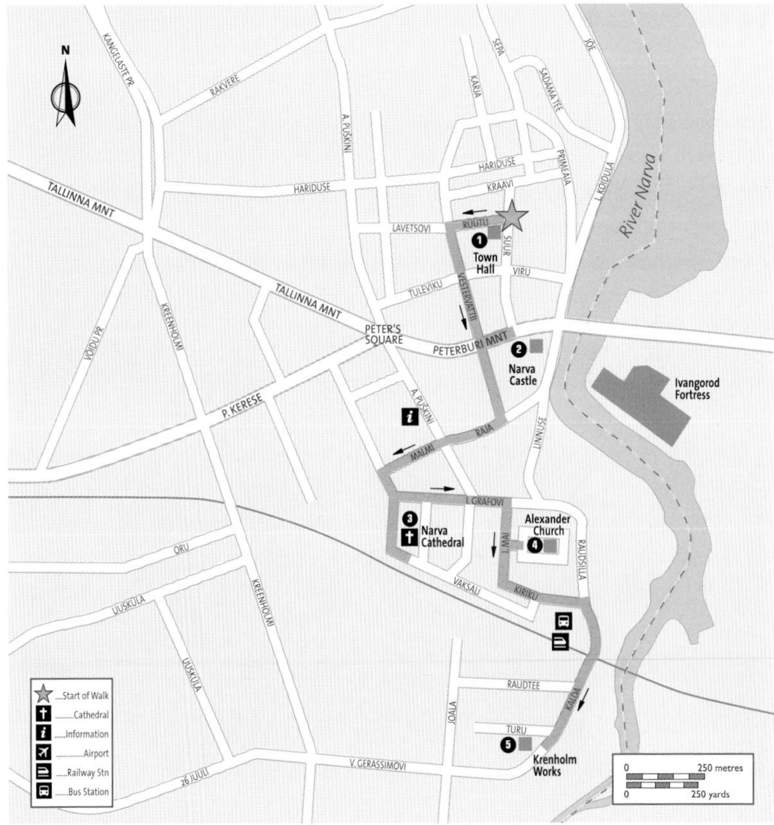

The Setu

The region of Southern Estonia, south and east of Põlva and Võru – called the Setumaa, or 'land of the Setu' – has perhaps the most ancient cultural tradition in Estonia, traces of which are still part of the lives of people here. This land is part of the national folklore of Estonia and features in fairy tales about the forest. The Estonian Setu, as the people of the region are called, have kept their distinctive Finno-Ugric dialect alive; their colourful costumes (though now worn mainly on special occasions and not commonly used as everyday gear) also date back several centuries. The Setu, who now number only around 10,000, have a rich folklore that centres on the 8,000-line epic poem, the *Pekolano*, which is sung aloud: it recounts the legends of their distant past. Their traditions frequently refer to a pagan fertility deity, Peko, and to a long-lost Setu king who slumbers in a cave of sand. Although nominally of the Russian Orthodox faith, since conversion to Christianity as recently as the 16th century, they managed to keep alive pagan ways much longer than their Estonian and Russian neighbours.

Typical of this merging of Christian and pagan traditions is the Setu community's biggest annual festival, which combines the Orthodox Transfiguration Day (19 August) with

Celebrations during a traditional Setu wedding

Setu costume

the proclamation of the Day of the Setu Kingdom (around 20 August). One of the men is chosen to be the *ulemtsootska* – a stand-in for the absent, sleeping king. There are competitions to find the finest singer. People dress in their traditional finery, which for the women includes dark red dresses, elaborate lace and massive silver necklaces and breastplates. Traditionally, these would be buried with the owner on her death, but today they are more likely to become valued heirlooms. This unique annual festival ends with visits to family graves, where token gifts of food and drink are left for the dead so that they too may enjoy the festivities.

Songs accompany the Setu from the cradle to the grave. Setu women are the main guardians of a treasury of songs that celebrate every aspect of life: weaving and sewing, herding flocks, bridal laments and songs for births, funerals and the turning of the seasons.

Unlike typical Estonian choirs, Setu *Leelo* epic choirs employ many harmonising voices, led by a strong female singer. One of the longest-established choirs is Leiko, a group which since it was founded in 1964 has recorded around 100 traditional songs and has performed at song festivals worldwide.

The Setu are a rural people, and a visit to one of their huddled villages of thatched wooden cottages and neat farmsteads is like taking a step back in time – Estonia reached these backwaters only in 1962. The Setu live in both Russia and Estonia, and their communities and families have been divided by the restrictions on cross-border travel since Estonia split from the Soviet Union. Some 3,000 Setu-speakers, belonging to 4 of the 12 *nulks* or clans that make up the Setu nation, were stranded on the Russian side of the border when Estonia and Russia ratified their new border in 2005.

Southern Estonia

Stretching from the shores of one of Europe's largest bodies of water to the Latvian border, Southern Estonia is a land of tranquil lakes, rivers and forests, fertile farmland and historic towns – among them, Estonia's second largest city. This is, too, a region studded with heritage sights that span centuries of Estonian history. Although the south is, in a very real sense, Estonia's true heartland, it sees surprisingly few foreign visitors.

Estonians, however, love their forest-covered southern hinterland, and are drawn to it in considerable numbers all year round; in summer, to cycle on its rolling country roads and swim and fish in its lakes and rivers, and in winter to ski on its snowy trails and hunt in its forests.

Though it may cause visitors some amusement, Estonians regard the south as their hill country. The Otepää hills, Estonia's favourite winter-sports resort, rise to more than 200m (656ft) above sea level. The country's highest summit, Suur-Munamägi, soars to a towering 318m (1,043ft).

Obinitsa

Obinitsa is a peaceful market town that lies at the heart of the Setumaa, home of a unique culture that preserves many of its old songs and customs. The town also houses a heritage museum. On the outskirts of town, next to a bathing lake, the tall granite statue of the Setu Song-Mother (Lauluima) is a local landmark that honours the singers who have done so much to keep the Setu oral tradition alive.

25km (16 miles) east of Võru.

Setu Heritage Museum

The museum highlights the culture of the Setu people of Estonia, with displays of beautiful folk costumes and other handicrafts, icons and woodcarving.

Signposted from town centre.

Tel: (372) 785 4190. Open: May–Sept Tue–Sun 11am–5pm. Admission charge.

Otepää

Otepää, Estonia's winter-sports capital, is surrounded by cross-country ski trails and toboggan runs. The hills that surround the town rise to little more than 200m (656ft) in altitude, but are thickly covered with snow in Estonia's chilly winters, and offer undemanding slopes of only around 150–250m (492–820ft) in length. Winter sports are enlivened when there are even six hours of daylight. Otepää is also the starting point for the annual cross-country ski

marathon held in early February, and for moto-cross marathons and cycle races in summer. While Otepää really comes into its own in winter, it is also a pleasant place to visit in summer, with outdoor activities including walking, fishing for trout, pike and perch, and cycling. Pühäjarve (Holy Lake), on the western outskirts of Otepää, has sand and pebble beaches and is popular with swimmers in summer. In mid-July it is the venue of the annual Beach Party, Estonia's top outdoor rock music event, which attracts more than 20,000 visitors.
70km (43 miles) south of Tartu.

Otepää Adventure Park
This open-air activity centre offers walking trails, mountain biking, adventure trails, climbing frames and nets and other activities for children and teenagers.

Southern Estonia

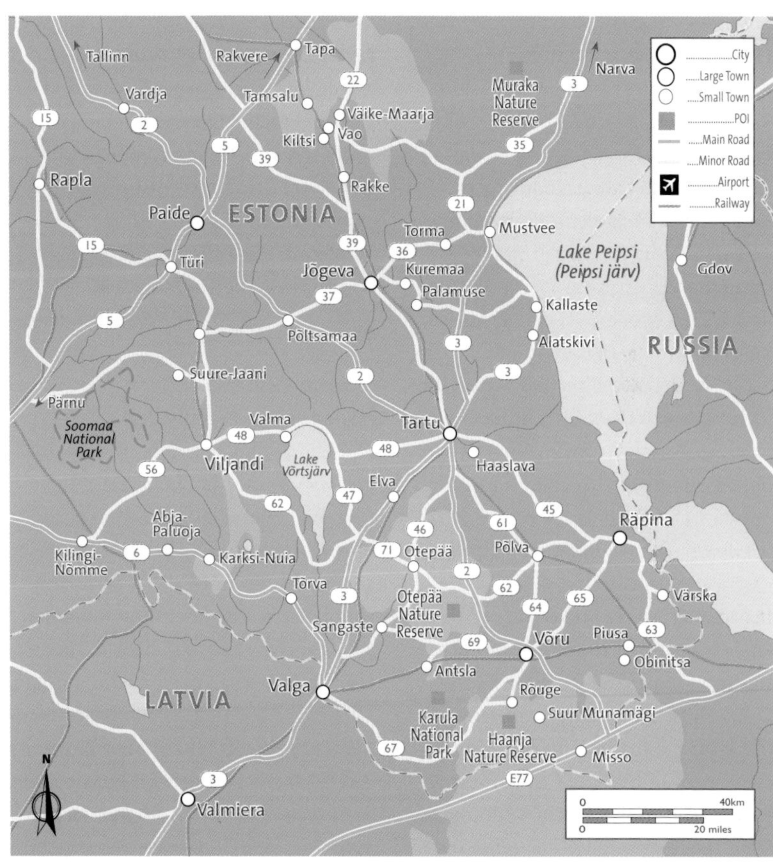

Farmsteads around Otepää town

Otepää Seikluspark. Tel: (372) 504 9783. Open: May–Sept daily 9am–7pm. Admission charge.

Paide

Paide is a pleasantly tranquil market town midway between Tallinn and Tartu. It has its own array of 19th-century architecture around the town hall square, overlooked by a medieval tower, known as Pikk Hermann, like its counterparts in Tallinn and Narva. The tower is worth climbing for the panorama of the town and countryside, but Paide's main attraction is its eclectic museum, founded in 1905.
95km (59 miles) northwest of Tartu.

Järvamaa County Museum

Paide is proud of its museum, which was set up in 1905 by the town's mayor, Oskar Brasche. Brasche bequeathed to the town the fixtures, fittings and equipment of his family's pharmacy, which dates from the mid-18th century. After the renovation of the museum in the year 2000, this venerable apothecary's establishment is still a highlight. Other facets of this quirky museum include a working-class living room from the 1950s, complete with Soviet-era accoutrements, and a 19th-century photographer's studio.
Lembitu 5. Tel: (372) 385 0276. www.jarva.ee/muuseum. Open: Wed–Sun 11am–6 pm. Admission charge.

Metsamoori Perepark (Woods Crone Family Park)

Sometimes also called the 'forest fairy', the woods crone is a benevolent figure from Estonian folklore and a repository of traditional healing lore. Children and adults can learn about herbs and wild flowers, take boat trips and learn about ancient Estonian beliefs. There is also farmhouse accommodation on site.
Vartemae Farm, Karula National Park, Mahkli, 43km (27 miles) west of Võru. Tel: (373) 786 7633 or (372) 5345 4222. www.metsamoor.ee. Open: May–Sept daily 9am–8pm. Admission charge.

Piusa Sand Caves

The legendary king of the Setu is believed to slumber through the centuries in a cavern of sand. These man-made caves, however, are too recent to be the royal bedchamber, as it is a relic of half a century of sand-mining which ended in 1970. The sand deposited by the Piusa River was used in the glass manufacturing industry. After sand-quarrying ceased, thousands of bats adopted the deserted pits as a roosting and breeding site, and in 1999 this post-industrial, sandy habitat was designated a nature reserve, protecting the largest bat colony in the Baltic region along with a range of rare plants, insects and reptiles.

5km (3 miles) north of Obinitsa. Open: daily 24hrs. Admission free.

Seto Farm Museum

The Seto Farm Museum reveals Estonian farm life from the late 19th and early 20th centuries, with old farm buildings, tools and costumes, and folklore performances.

Pikk 40, Värska village. Tel: (372) 505 4673. www.hot.ee/setomuuseum. Open: May–Sept daily 10am–5pm; Oct–Apr Tue–Sat 10am–4pm.

Suur Munamägi

In almost any other country, 318m- (1,043ft) tall Suur Munamägi would be regarded as no more than a hillock. In low-lying Estonia, it is revered as the country's highest summit. For those who wish to climb to the top of this awesome geographical feature, a path starts from just outside the village of Haanja and leads through pine woods to the Vaatetorn viewing tower, a walk that takes less than ten minutes.

12km (7 miles) south of Võru. Tel: (372) 786 7514 or 787 8847. Viewing tower open: Nov–mid-Apr Sat–Sun noon–3pm; mid-Apr–Aug daily 10am–8pm; Sept daily 10am–5pm; Oct Sat–Sun 10am–5pm. Admission charge.

Tartu

Estonia's second city, on the banks of the Emajõgi River, has a population of over 100,000 and will celebrate its 1,000th anniversary in 2030.

Tartu, known until the first period of Estonian independence as Dorpat, owes much to the merchants of the Hanseatic League, who brought wealth and trade to the city, and to King Gustav II Adolph of Sweden, who founded its university in 1632. A new statue of the King, erected in 1992, pays tribute to his role.

The University became the powerhouse of Estonia's intellectual and cultural life, playing a key part in fostering a national culture and literature in the 19th and 20th centuries. Its 15,000-strong student body makes Tartu one of Estonia's liveliest and most youthful cities.

The cobbled Raekoja plats (Town Hall Square) is the hub of a historic town centre, and is dominated by 18th-century buildings, including the colourful Town Hall, with its ochre and mauve livery, on the west side of the

Tartu Town Hall

cobbled square. Many older buildings were made of wood, and much of the old town was destroyed by fire in 1775, after which it was extensively rebuilt in more durable materials. World War II destroyed most of the remaining wooden buildings.

Tartu has more than 20 museums and art galleries, several of them under the auspices of various University departments. Some should not be missed; others are really interesting only to specialists.
200km (124 miles) southeast of Tallinn. Buses from Tallinn every 30mins, take 2hrs 30mins nonstop. 2 trains daily from Tallinn, taking around 4hrs.

A Le Coq Beer Museum

Tartu is the home of one of Estonia's biggest breweries, which produces the popular A Le Coq lager brand (originally brought to Estonia by an Englishman in the late 19th century). The exhibition consists of five floors displaying several hundred items of brewing and bottling equipment and other aspects of the brewer's trade, and the guided tour concludes with a sampling session.
Tähtvere 56/62. Tel: (372) 744 9711. www.alecoq.ee. Tours: Thur 2pm & Sat 10am, noon and 2pm. Admission charge.

City Museum

Tartu City Museum is housed in one of the city's most attractive historic buildings, built in 1790. Worth seeing are the scale model of Tartu in 1940, before the destruction wrought by bombing in World War II, and a collection of glassware, silver, clocks and textiles from the 17th-century heyday of Swedish rule in Estonia.
Narva mantee 23. Tel: (372) 746 1911. http://linnamuuseum.tartu.ee. Open: Tue–Sun 11am–6pm. Admission charge.

Estonian National Museum

Founded in 1909, the Estonian National Museum has extensive and colourful

displays of traditional Estonian and Setu costumes, handicrafts and photographs. Also highlighted are the histories of other nationalities whose history is bound up with Estonia: Imperial and Soviet Russians, Baltic Germans and Swedes.
Kuperjanovi 9, but due for relocation to new site at Raadi manor outside Tartu by early 2009. Tel: (372) 742 1311. www.erm.ee. Open: Wed–Sun 11am–6pm. Admission charge, except Fri.

KGB Cells Museum
Offering a chilling reminder of life in the not so distant past, this was the local headquarters of the notorious Committee for State Security, as the Soviet secret police was known. The prison cells are preserved as they were before the collapse of the USSR, and photographs and documents perpetuate the memory of Estonians tortured, executed or sent to the prison camps of the USSR's Gulag archipelago by the KGB.
Riia 15b. Tel: (372) 746 1717. http://linnamuuseum.tartu.ee. Open: Tue–Sat 11am–4pm. Admission charge.

Nineteenth-Century Tartu Citizen's Home Museum
This collection is an annexe of the City Museum, and replicates the private and everyday life of a middle-class home of the 1830s. The living room, dining room, the owner's study and bedroom are furnished in the German-influenced Biedermeier style typical of the period.
Jaani 16. Tel: (372) 736 1545. http://linnamuuseum.tartu.ee. Open: Wed–Sun 11am–6pm. Admission charge.

Old wooden house at Supalinn, on the outskirts of Tartu

Oskar Luts Museum

This was the Tartu home of the revered Estonian pharmacist and writer Oskar Luts (1887–1953), whose works depicted life at the beginning of the 20th century in Estonian villages and towns. There is a permanent exhibition devoted to his life and work.
Riia 38. Tel: (372) 746 1030. http://linnamuuseum.tartu.ee. Open: Wed–Sat 11am–5pm, Sun 1–5pm. Admission charge.

Jaani Kirk (St John's Church)

The St John's Church or Jaani Kirk is a splendid example of medieval northern Gothic architecture, with its square brick bell tower, dating from the 14th century, and unique terracotta sculptures. Many of these were damaged or destroyed during World War II, and the church as a whole was neglected until 1989, when restoration began. Around 1,000 of the 2,000 original images of saints and martyrs have now been replaced or restored. The church's copper steeple and its bells were restored in 1999.
Lutsu 16-3, Tartu. Tel: (372) 744 2229. email: tartu.jaani@eelk.ee. Open: Mon–Sat 10am–7pm, Sun 10am–1pm. Admission charge. Tower open: Mon and Fri 12.30–7pm, Wed, Thur and Sat 11am–7pm. Admission charge.

Museum of Song Festivals

Tartu's newest museum, opened in autumn 2007, tells the story of the country's tradition of song festivals and massed choirs, through centuries of occupation to the 'Singing Revolution' of 1988 and the present day.
Jaani 14. Tel: (372) 746 911. Open: Apr–Sept Wed–Sun 11am–6pm; Oct–Mar Wed–Sun 10am–3pm.

Tartu University

St John's Church is a wonderful example of medieval Gothic architecture

Tartu Art Museum

This crooked old mansion on the east side of Town Hall Square was once the home of General Mikhail Barclay de Tolly (1761–1818), one of the architects of the defeat of Napoleon Bonaparte's invasion of Russia in 1812. It now houses a comprehensive portfolio of hundreds of works by modern and contemporary Estonian artists and an ever-changing array of temporary exhibitions.

Raekoja plats 18. Tel: (372) 744 1080. www.tartmus.ee. Open: Wed–Sun 11am–6pm. Admission charge.

Tartu University Art Museum

This museum, formerly known as the Museum of Classical Antiquity, has been confusingly renamed. The oldest museum in Estonia, founded in 1803, its collection is mainly composed of copies of classical Greek sculpture, along with a few Egyptian sarcophagi. More interesting and locally relevant are the hundreds of fine Russian Orthodox icons.

Ülikooli 18. Tel: (372) 737 5384. www.ut.ee/artmuseum. Open: Mon–Fri 11am–5pm. Admission charge. Guided tours: Sat & Sun by advance reservation only.

Tartu University Botanical Garden

Founded in 1803, the university's botanical garden boasts 57 species of palm tree, housed in the highest greenhouse in the Baltic countries. Arguably of more interest to the visitor is the garden of native Estonian plants.

Lai 38/40. Tel: (372) 737 6180. www.ut.ee/botaed. Open: daily 10am–5pm. Admission charge.

Tartu University History Museum

The museum highlights the history of the city and its museum from its foundation in 1603 until the present day. Its displays include paintings and photographs of highlights from

The recently renovated Alatskivi Castle

history. The museum is housed in the former Sts Peter and Paul Cathedral, an imposing 13th-century building which was much damaged during the conflicts of the 16th and 17th centuries and lay in ruins until restoration by the University in the 19th century.
Lossi 25. Tel: (372) 737 5677. www.ut.ee/ajaloomuuseum. Open: Wed–Sun 11am–5pm. Admission charge.

Toy Museum

This comprehensive and charming collection of toys, dolls and puppets will delight children and adults too. There are puppets from all over the world, traditional dolls from Finland, Hungary and Estonia, and elaborate stage marionettes, along with a working model railway.
Lutsu 8. Tel: (372) 746 1777. www.mm.ee. Open: daily 10am–5pm. Admission charge.

Tartu environs

Around Tartu city lies a diverse region of river valleys, forests and wetlands, lying between Estonia's largest lakes – Lake Peipsi and Lake Võrtsjärv. The county is dotted with old manor houses and picturesque villages, and Lake Peipsi – scene of a historic battle between the forces of Prince Alexander Nevsky of Kiev and the Teutonic Knights of the Livonian Order – is one of Estonia's grandest natural spectacles.

Alatskivi Castle

This mock-medieval, 19th-century stately home looks amusingly incongruous in its Estonian setting, as well it may as its owner and architect, Arved von Nolcken, borrowed the design of Balmoral Castle, Scottish home of Queen Victoria, which had impressed him on a visit to Britain in the 1870s. It was completed in 1885. Used as the headquarters of a collective

farm during the Soviet period, its interior has benefited from a renovation programme that was completed in 2005, giving it back some of its grandeur.
8km (5 miles) south of Kallaste village, 60km (37 miles) southeast of Tallinn.

Lake Peipsi
Lake Peipsi, the largest body of water in Estonia and the fourth largest in Europe, covers an area of 3,555sq km (1,373sq miles) and is scenically beautiful, culturally interesting, yet remarkably little visited. In part, this is because its location, on the frontier between Estonia and Russia, made it a sensitive security zone in the days of the USSR. The border between Estonia and Russia remained uncertain until 2005, so there was little incentive to invest in tourism infrastructure, or to promote Peipsi's undeniable attractions. Those who make the effort to reach the lake will find much that is appealing, including uncrowded sandy beaches for summer swimming and sunbathing, small fishing villages, reedbeds, marshes and lakeside woodlands that shelter populations of water birds, fish and larger mammals.

During the 13th century, Peipsi was the scene of one of the decisive battles that shaped the history of the Baltic region, when the Slavic prince Alexander Nevsky of Novgorod defeated the Teutonic Knights of the Livonian Order in a battle fought on the frozen surface of the lake in midwinter. This historic clash was immortalised on celluloid by the Soviet director Sergei Eisenstein in the 1938 film *Alexander Nevsky*.

Lake Peipsi, the largest body of water in Estonia

Lake Võrtsjärv is Estonia's second-largest lake

Since the 18th century, the Estonian shore of Lake Peipsi has been home to communities of Old Believers, a Christian sect whose traditions set them apart from the Russian Orthodox Church and who moved to the western borderlands of the Russian Empire to evade religious persecution. Their villages, including Kasepää, Raja, Nina, Varna and Kolkja, stretch for many kilometres along the shore of the lake. Peipsi's largest fishing village, Kallaste, also has a fine sandy beach which attracts many Estonian visitors in the summer months.
30km (19 miles) east of Tartu.

Lake Võrtsjärv
Estonia's second-biggest lake is 40km (25 miles) long; with a surface area of 270sq km (104sq miles), it is the largest lake lying completely within Estonia. At its deepest, Võrtsjärv is only 6m (20ft) deep. The Emajõgi River flows from Võrtsjärv eastwards into Lake Peipsi, passing through Peipsi town on its way.

Tartu Aviation Museum
More than 200 model aircraft are displayed in the indoor section of this museum, which is dedicated to the history of aviation in Estonia and worldwide. Parked outside are examples of the real thing, including Soviet-built MiG-21MF and Su-22M4 fighters, a TS-11 Iskra trainer, Mi-8 and Mi-2RL helicopters, a French Mirage IIIRS, a Swedish Viggen-37, and more. Though it is called the Tartu Aviation Museum, it is actually at Haaslava village.
27km (17 miles) from Tartu at Lange küla, Haaslava. Tel: (372) 740 9680. www.lennundusmuuseum.ee.

Open: May–Sept daily 10am–6pm; Oct daily 10am–5pm; Apr & Nov, dependent on weather (call to confirm). Admission charge.

Torma

Torma is the centre of Estonia's brass band tradition, stemming from 1848, when a local man, Adam Jakobson (1817–57), put together the first brass band ever formed in Estonia. Ever since, this small farming town has kept brass music alive, and since 2000 it has been the venue for ToPoF, an annual brass band festival that commemorates Jakobson's contribution to the world of music and attracts brass bands and musicians from as far away as southern Portugal.
22km (14 miles) northeast of Jõgeva.

Türi

Nicknamed Estonia's 'spring capital', Türi is proud of its public and private gardens, and in early summer its numerous green spaces are filled with flowers. The town is an interesting mix of old and new, with a local museum that highlights its role in the modernisation and industrialisation of Estonia in the first half of the 20th century – when Türi was the hub of the Estonian railway system – along with historic buildings from as far back as the 13th century.
20km (12 miles) south of Paide.

St Martin's Church

This pretty 13th-century church is noted for its chapel and spire, and stained-glass windows by the

An exhibit at Tartu Aviation Museum

St John's Church in Viljandi was reconsecrated in 1992

artist Dolores Hoffmann.
Weidemanni 9. Tel: (372) 387 8330. www.tyri.ee. Open: May–Sept Wed–Sun 10am–1pm & 3–6 pm.

Türi Museum
The Türi Museum highlights the development of the Estonian railway system in the 19th and 20th centuries and also has displays of memorabilia from the town's industrial past. Housed in the same premises is the **Estonian Broadcasting Museum**, with an exhibition of early radios, TVs and other paraphernalia of the airwaves.
Vabriku pst. 11. Tel: (372) 385 7429. www.hot.ee/tyrimuuseum. Open: Tue–Sat 10am–5pm. Admission charge.

Valga
The little town of Valga is next to the border between Estonia and its southern neighbour, Latvia. The border here is defined by a stream that is little more than a roadside ditch that narrowly separates Valga from Valka, on the Latvian side of the frontier. Valga lies on the main railway line between Tallinn and Rīga (capital of Latvia), and points west. There is not much here to detain the visitor, apart from the **Valga County Museum**, with its wax figures, old Estonian banknotes and coins, and bits and pieces from the town's 19th-century bank.
80km (50 miles) southwest of Tartu. Valga Museum: Vabaduse 8. Tel: (372) 766 8863. www.valgamuseum.ee. Open: Wed–Sat 10am–5pm. Admission charge

Viljandi
Viljandi, on the shore of Lake Viljandi, is a peaceful market town at the heart of one of Estonia's most fertile agricultural areas. Despite being devastated by Swedish, Polish, German and Russian armies for over four centuries of conflict, and the destruction wrought to its traditional wooden buildings by repeated fires in 1682, 1765, 1894 and 1905, many of its more important buildings have survived. Founded in the 12th century, the town is dominated by the ruins of a 13th-century castle built by the Livonian Order. Other noteworthy buildings include St John's Church, a former Franciscan abbey that was reconsecrated as a Lutheran place of worship after renovation in 1992. St John's has some beautiful new stained-glass windows. St Paul's Lutheran Church is a red-brick pseudo-Gothic building with a fine altar painting of Christ on the Cross by the Dresden religious artist Carl Andrea, dating from 1866.

Viljandi environs
The Viljandi region is dominated by the Sakala Uplands, a region of picturesque, heavily wooded river valleys, including the valleys of the Viljandi and Pärnu rivers. To the west,

The surviving ruins of Viljandi Castle

this hill country gives way to low-lying forested plains and marshland. One of the region's natural wonders is the Viiralti Oak, which is reckoned to be Estonia's oldest tree. It has become a symbol of the country's pristine environment. Several centuries old, the tree gets its name from the well-known Estonian artist Eduard Viiralt, who depicted it in his painting *The Landscape of Viljandimaa.*

Soomaa National Park

Soomaa National Park, roughly midway between Viljandi and Pärnu, was established in 1993 to protect Estonia's widest expanse of wetlands, woods and water meadows. The park provides a refuge for a wide range of wildlife, including beaver, elk and a number of birds, plants and insects that are found nowhere else in Estonia. Soomaa is the only place in Europe where dugout canoes, made from a single log, are still in use.

25km (16 miles) west of Viljandi. Soomaa National Park Visitor Centre, Kortsi-Toramaa, Viljandimaa. Tel: (372) 435 7164. www.soomaa.ee. Open: Tue–Sun 10am–6pm. Admission free.

Võru

Founded in 1784 during the reign of Catherine the Great, Võru seems in many ways much more modern than many rural Estonian towns, with streets laid out in a grid pattern that reveals it as a planned community, albeit one dating from the late 18th century. The old, wooden buildings of the original settlement are surrounded by less charming modern suburbs. Võru is best known to Estonians as the home of F R Kreutzwald, creator of the national epic, the *Kalevipoeg*.

F R Kreutzwald Memorial Museum

The museum is dedicated to the life and works of Friedrich Reinhold Kreutzwald, who lived and worked here as a doctor while compiling the folk tales that eventually became the *Kalevipoeg*. It also includes an outdoor exhibition of sculptures inspired by his poetry.

Kreutzwaldi 31. Tel: (372) 782 1798. www.hot.ee/muuseumvoru. Open: May–Sept Wed–Sun 10am–6pm; Oct–Apr Wed–Sun 10am–5pm. Admission charge.

F R KREUTZWALD

Despite his Teutonic-sounding name, Friedrich Reinhold Kreutzwald was born into an Estonian peasant family. A talented scholar, he trained as a doctor at Tartu University and set up his own practice in Võru in 1833. He then began collecting local folk tales and ballads, which he brought together to create what is still regarded as Estonia's national epic, the *Kalevipoeg* – although it is now known that Kreutzwald made most of it up.

A wildlife signboard in Soomaa National Park

F R Kreutzwald and the *Kalevipoeg*

A statue of Kalevipoeg (Son of Kalev) in Tartu's riverside park symbolises the soldiers of Estonia's 1918–20 War of Independence

Is Estonia's national epic a fraud? Few Estonians would agree. The *Kalevipoeg* (*Son of Kalev*) is universally revered as one of the first symbols of Estonia's cultural revival in the 19th century. But the truth is that the poem is a mixture of genuine ancestral myths and legends, blended by its creator with a great deal of invented material.

Inspired by the Finnish epic, the *Kalevala* – which itself is a 19th-century creation, cobbled together by the Finnish poet and collector of folk tales, Elias Lönnrot, from many fragments of traditional song and verse – the *Kalevipoeg* is the work of Friedrich Reinhold Kreutzwald (1803–82). It tells the story of a half-mythical Estonian warrior-king, his victories and his eventual death – but as no English translation is available, it is impossible for non-Estonians to judge the poem on its merits.

Despite his Germanic name, Kreutzwald was no Baltic baron but the son of a peasant family from Joepere near Rakvere who made it his life's work to collect and preserve Estonian folklore. His is a story of rags to modest prosperity. Educated at a village school, he earned enough as a tutor to the children of well-off Tallinn and St Petersburg families to enrol at the University of Tartu, where he studied medicine. After graduating, he became a small-town doctor in Võru in 1833.

At university, Kreutzwald was one of a circle of students and academics who were fired by the dream of creating an authentic Estonian culture, and for the next 20 years Kreutzwald worked in his spare time to fuse the folk myths with the products of his own imagination to create the *Kalevipoeg*. The work was first published in a series of episodes over two years between 1857 and 1859, making Kreutzwald famous and earning itself a niche at the heart of Estonian culture – never mind that most of it is made up.

Kreutzwald became an inspiration to generations of Estonian writers and cultural nationalists, including the poet Lydia Koidula, with whom he maintained a lengthy correspondence until her marriage to a Latvian doctor who spoke no Estonian. Kreutzwald saw her decision as cultural treason, and ended their correspondence. Despite this, Kreutzwald saw nothing wrong in learning the German language, which in his day was still the language of the educated classes in Estonia, in order to further his career.

And that proved to be a wise decision. Despite its popularity, Kreutzwald profited very little from the publication of the *Kalevipoeg* and made his living as a local doctor until his retirement in 1877. His former home and surgery in Võru, in southern Estonia, is now a museum dedicated to his life, with a gallery of works of art inspired by Estonia's national epic.

Friedrich Reinhold Kreutzwald

Walk: Around Tartu's Old Town

The Old Town is compact, with the Emajõgi River forming its eastern boundary and the ruins of the Dom or Cathedral to the west. There is plenty to see, for the town centre is dotted with historic buildings and monuments, of special interest to scholars and artists.

Distance: 3.5km (2¼ miles).

Time: 3–4 hours for the full walk, including visits to the museums.

There are plenty of lively cafés and bars in the old town and the city centre. Start with a stroll around Raekoja plats (Town Hall Square), formerly the town's main market square.

1 Town Hall

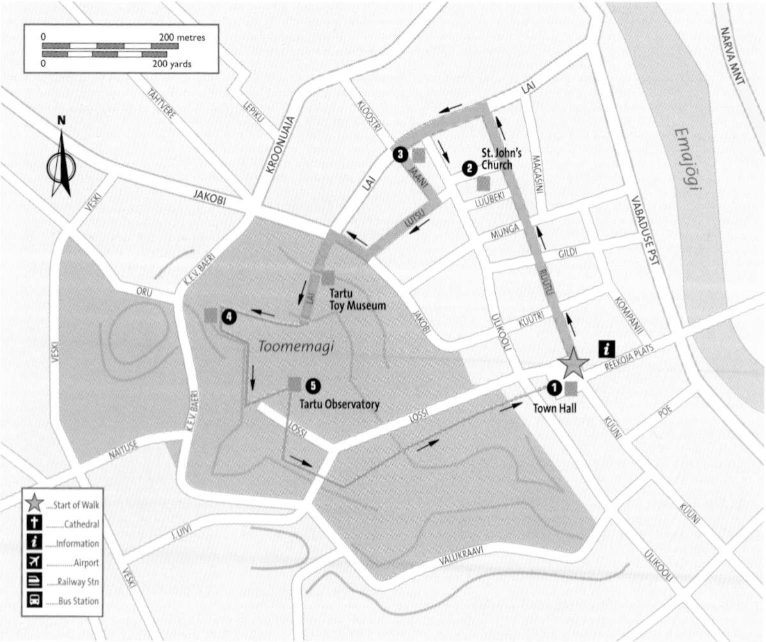

The square is dominated by the Town Hall, which was completed in 1786, the work of the German architect, J H Walter. The building is the third to stand on the site, two earlier town halls having been destroyed by fire in the 17th and 18th centuries. The fountain and statue of the 'Kissing Students' was placed in front of the Town Hall in 1998 and has become a symbol of the city. Another building worth noting on the square is the 'slanted house' at No 18. Originally the home of the Barclay de Tolly family, it now houses the Art Museum of Tartu. No 2 Town Hall Square has a striking rococo and late baroque façade.

From Town Hall Square, walk north along Rüütli, the main street of the Old Town, to St John's Church.

2 St John's Church

St John's Church is one of the finest examples of the northern Gothic style. Built during the early 14th century, it was damaged during World War II and has only recently been restored.

Turn left at the corner of Lai and Rüütli, then left again on Jaani, a street with a number of restored historic buildings, including some wooden houses which survived the fire that devastated the city in 1775.

3 Jaani street

Two restored houses worth noting on Jaani are the Tampere House, at No 4, and the Uppsala House, at No 7. Tartu has had close links with Tampere in Finland, and with the Swedish university city of Uppsala since the 17th century. At No 16 is the Museum of the 19th-century Citizen's Home.

From the Museum, turn west on Lutsu and walk towards Toomemagi (Dome Hill), turning right at the corner of Lutsu and Jakobi. Enter the park from the gate on the corner.

4 Toomemagi

The ruins of the cathedral, which was destroyed by fire in 1624, and the castle, which was abandoned at the end of the Great Northern War, are surrounded by well-groomed gardens laid out at the beginning of the 19th century. Passing the Tartu Toy Museum, note the monument to K E von Baer at the foot of the Dome Hill. Baer (1792–1876) studied at Tartu University before going on to lead expeditions to the Arctic Circle and Caspian Sea, and was one of the first modern anthropologists. Turn right, and continue around the hill to the statue of Kristjan Jaak (Christian Jacob) Peterson, one of the founders of modern Estonian literature and a graduate of Tartu University.

Follow the path anticlockwise past the picturesque ruined arches of the cathedral, and cross the ornamental 'Angel's Bridge', built in 1838.

Follow the path on to the Observatory.

5 Tartu Observatory

Tartu's historic Observatory, built in 1810, boasted the world's largest lens telescope. It is now an astronomical museum. The path leads back to Ülikooli and Town Hall Square.

Drive: Manor houses of Virumaa

The Virumaa region, straddling North and South Estonia, was a heartland of the Baltic-German community. Until independence in 1918, this rich farmland was divided into large estates owned by wealthy landowning families. Their lands were nationalised soon after independence, and almost all left for Germany, but their castles and manors remain.

Distance: 50km (31 miles). Time: Around 8 hours.

This drive starts at Rakvere, on highway 22. From here, drive south for 15km (9 miles), then turn right to Porkuni and its ruined manor.

1 Porkuni Manor

A 15th-century gate tower is the only surviving part of the original Baltic-German stronghold that stood here. Next to it, a newer manor was built in 1869 by the von Rennenkampf family. The tower houses a unique geological collection in the Limestone Museum.
From Porkuni, return to highway 22 and drive south for 10km (6 miles) to Väike-Maarja.

2 Väike-Maarja

The Gothic stronghold-church of Väike-Maarja was built in the late 14th century and has striking stained-glass windows, and members of many of the region's prominent Baltic-German families are buried in its cemetery. At Pikk 10 the Väike-Maarja Museum is one of the few in Estonia that reflects the Soviet era in a more positive light.
Drive 4km (2½ miles) south from Väike-Maarja and turn west, off route 22, to Kiltsi.

3 Kiltsi Manor

Kiltsi is one of the earliest Baltic-German strongholds, with an 18th-century manor built on the site of a 14th-century castle. In the 19th century it became the home of the von Krusensterns, one of the most influential Estonian dynasties during the Imperial Russian period.
Drive 1km (2/3 mile) north from Kiltsi to Vao Manor, signposted from Kiltsi.

4 Vao Manor

Vao's limestone keep dates from the early 15th century and contains a small exhibition introducing the history of the manor and its owners, the von Rennenkampfs, who were among Estonia's wealthiest landowners.

Return to route 22, cross the highway and follow a country road east for about 8km (5 miles) to reach Simuna.

5 Simuna

Simuna dates from the 13th century and is one of Estonia's oldest religious foundations. It was enlarged and made into a three-naved church in the mid-15th century.

Drive east through Simuna village and Laekvere. 4km (2½ miles) east of Laekvere, turn left (north) on route 21. 4km (2½ miles) north, turn right to Muuga Manor.

6 Muuga Manor

Muuga manor was built in neo-Renaissance style between 1866 and 1872 for the portraitist and landscape artist Carl Timoleon von Neff, who painted the Russian Imperial family and court and was curator of the Hermitage palace in St Petersburg.

From Muuga, follow highway 21 back to Rakvere.

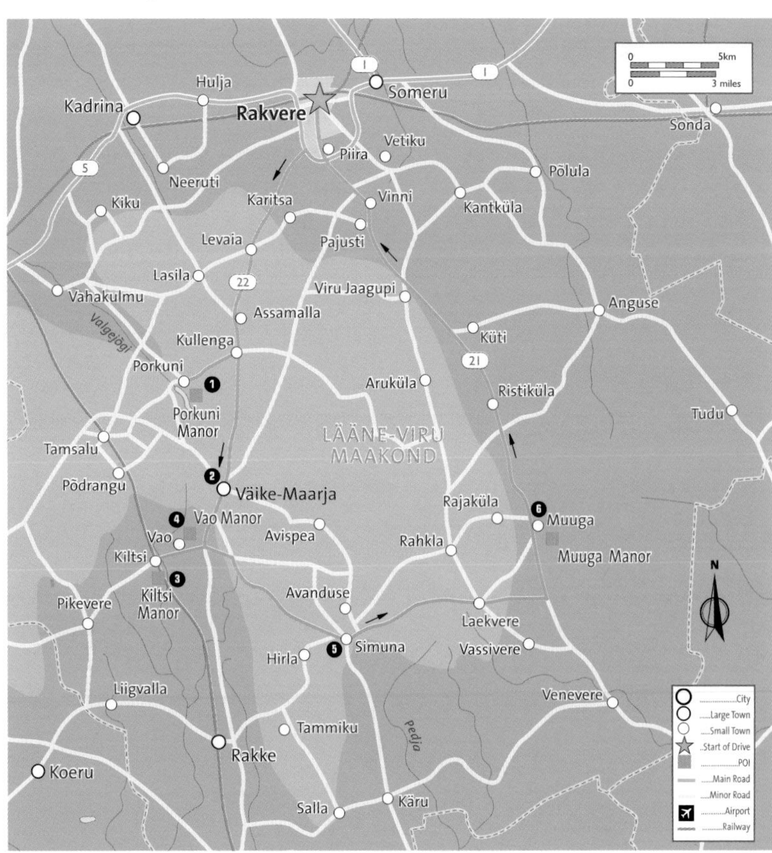

The Baltic Sea

Estonia's geography and its history have been shaped by the Baltic Sea, which is the largest body of brackish water in the world. Called *Läänemeri* (Western Sea) by Estonians, the Baltic has connected Estonian ports with Denmark, Sweden, Finland and Germany since early medieval times, laying the country open to a wide range of foreign influences and invaders. Fed by more than 250 rivers, the Baltic is much less salty than the world's oceans, so it freezes more readily in winter, with a long, slow thaw that prolongs Estonia's winters, while slow surface freezing also makes for a longer autumnal season.

Swedish Vikings opened Estonia's Baltic Sea coast to commerce in the 8th century AD, and for the next 12 centuries, half a dozen powers contended for control of the seas and ports.

Even though ice and frequent winter storms make the Baltic a hazardous sea for shipping, Estonia's ports – especially Tallinn, Narva, Haapsalu and Paldiski – were coveted

Baltic coastline at Lahemaa

by its neighbours, especially Russia, which lacked its own Baltic ports. Seizing these Estonian harbour cities was the main aim of Peter the Great's conquest of Estonia in the Great Northern War, and during the period of Soviet occupation Estonian ports were regarded as the USSR's most vital naval bases.

The Baltic is Europe's newest sea, and was formed less than 5,000 years ago, at the end of the last Ice Age. The melting of the ice that had covered Scandinavia left an inland sea which was separated from the North Sea by a stretch of land between Jutland (in modern Denmark) and Sweden. Around 4500 BC, rising seas breached this barrier, creating the Danish archipelago.

Estonia's islands, and much of mainland Estonia, emerged from beneath the waters of the Baltic even more recently. Along this section of the Baltic coast, the surface of the earth has been rising steadily ever since the retreat of the massive, heavy Ice Age glaciers. Geologists estimate that Estonia is rising at the rate of around 1m every 350 years, which in geological terms is an extremely rapid pace that could even offset the rise in Baltic sea levels that is being caused by global warming.

Fishing in the Baltic has declined, and many formerly valuable fish species such as cod, herring and salmon have been seriously overfished. However, Estonian fishermen still haul in herring, sprats, eel and flatfish from Estonia's national fishing zones.

The sea cliffs of Northern Estonia

The Baltic seabed is divided among the ten nations that surround it (Estonia, Latvia, Lithuania, Poland, Germany, Denmark, Norway, Sweden, Finland and Russia) and there has been undersea exploration for oil and gas reserves beneath the eastern Baltic.

The Baltic is almost entirely landlocked. At its narrowest, between Denmark and Sweden, the strait that eventually connects it with the North Sea is only a few kilometres wide. With many rivers carrying runoff from cities and industrial areas, the Baltic is very vulnerable to pollution, and threats to fisheries and marine wildlife have led to greater cooperation between Estonia and other Baltic nations on environmental protection.

Western Estonia

Estonia's western coast, facing the sheltered Gulf of Rīga, is one of the most attractive and little-visited stretches of the Baltic seashore. It stretches for more than 500km (311 miles) of rocky headlands, narrow inlets, bays and sandy beaches, from Haapsalu in the north to the Latvian border in the south. Offshore lie dozens of islands – some large, while others are little more than windswept rocks that are inhabited only by colonies of sea birds.

For most of its length, the west coast is sheltered from the open waters of the Baltic by two large islands, Saaremaa and Hiiumaa, and in summer the shallow waters of the Gulf of Rīga can be surprisingly warm, reaching sea temperatures as high as 21°C (70°F). The sandy beaches around Pärnu, the biggest and liveliest city in the region, are a very popular summer resort area for Estonians, and Pärnu becomes a real party town in July and August, when the long, light evenings encourage all-night celebrations. Pärnu is also a cultural centre, with regular performances and festivals of traditional and classical music.

Western Estonia is also rich in natural beauty, with nature reserves that shelter rare birds and unique coastal ecosystems. Inland, between the Pärnu and Vigala rivers, which flow westward into the Gulf of Rīga, are wide expanses of forest and wetlands. Offshore, the islands present a different landscape, of sand dunes, moorland and heath, and several islands are protected within designated maritime nature reserves.

HAAPSALU

Haapsalu is a town that has seen more than its fair share of the vicissitudes of history. Sitting on an excellent natural anchorage, it was strategically vital to every would-be conqueror of the region from its foundation in 1279 until the Soviet era, and suffered accordingly, being repeatedly besieged and bombarded by a variety of assailants. Peter the Great of Russia levelled the town and its fortifications in 1715 to deny it to his Swedish adversaries, and Haapsalu became almost a ghost town for more than a century. In the mid-19th century a local doctor, Carl Abraham Hunnius (1797–1851), popularised Haapsalu as a health resort, praising the remedial powers of the local mineral mud. It became a favoured resort for Russian aristocrats. During the second half of the 19th century, it was frequently visited by the

Russian royal family, setting the seal on its status as a fashionable summer retreat, and attracting luminaries such as the composer Pyotr Tchaikovsky, who wrote several pieces of music here. Haapsalu continued to flourish during Estonia's first spell of independence (1920–1940) and a scattering of grandiose villas and public buildings along its seafront are relics of that period. During the Soviet era, Haapsalu was within a military security zone and was off-limits to foreigners (including most Estonians). The last Russian troops left in 1945, and since then the town has begun to reassert itself as a summer resort, with sandy beaches and newly built or restored hotels, some of which still offer treatment programmes using Haapsalu's health-giving mud. The town has a few sights worth seeing, including a castle that has been demolished and rebuilt through the centuries. It is said to be haunted by a famous ghost, but for many visitors,

WILD BIRDS

Western Estonia is on one of Europe's most important bird migration routes, and in spring and autumn, as many as one million birds of hundreds of different species flock in and out of the area each day, passing through protected reserves including Vilsandi, on Saaremaa island, and Matsalu, near Haapsalu.

Western Estonia

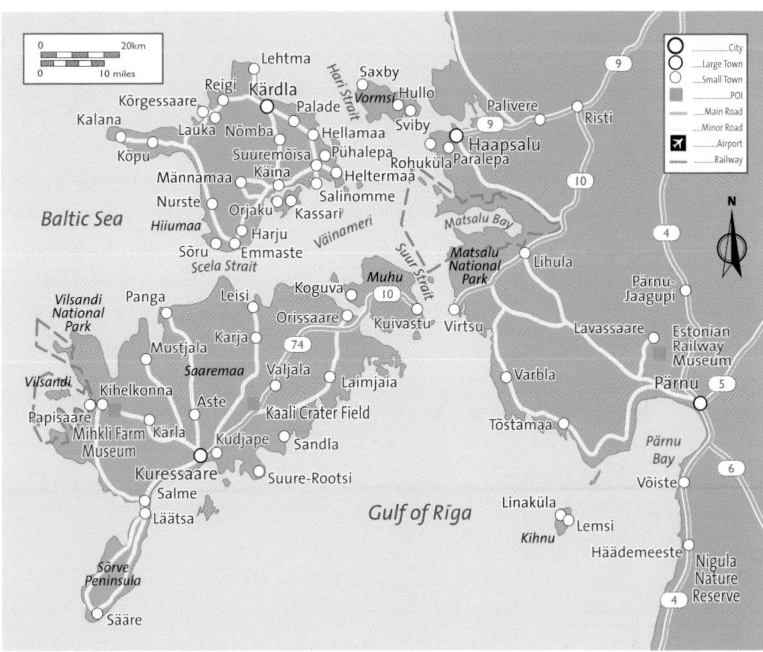

Haapsalu Castle Museum hosts the 'White Lady' festival

Haapsalu is most likely to be visited as part of a journey to the nearby island of Hiiumaa. Haapsalu is set on a 3km (1½-mile) long peninsula, which juts northward into Haapsalu laht (Haapsalu Bay), with beaches on either side. The beach east of the town is a source of the supposedly medicinal (and somewhat malodorous) black mud that gives Haapsalu its reputation as a health spa. For swimming in summer, Paralepa beach, west of the town centre, has more sand and is a better bet. Haapsalu is a small town, and its attractions are easily explored on foot.

Haapsalu Castle Museum

Haapsalu Castle Museum lies 120km (75 miles) southwest of Tallinn (two hours by bus). The castle, built as the seat of a 13th-century bishopric, is the venue of the annual 'White Lady' festival in August, when the ruined walls are lit up by sound and light performances. Some 800m (890yds) of dilapidated ramparts surround the ruins of the main castle, which, together with the imposing former cathedral, now house the Castle Museum. Within is an impressive array of wicked-looking 15th- and 16th-century swords, halberds, daggers and other implements of medieval mayhem. It is possible to ascend the watchtower for a panoramic view of Haapsalu and its surroundings.

Lossipark 1.

Castle park and ramparts: Open: daily 7am–9pm. Admission free. Castle Museum: Open: mid-May–mid-Sept Tue–Sun 10am–6pm. Admission charge.

Estonian Railway Museum

Sadly, Haapsalu no longer has a passenger railway service, but its former

railway station is a memorial to the town's heyday as a summer resort for the Imperial Russian aristocracy. It opened in 1905, when the railway line from St Petersburg to Tallinn was extended to Haapsalu, putting the town firmly on the 20th-century map. It was designed specifically to meet the rarefied needs of Russian royalty, with a 200m (656ft) roof covering its platform to ensure that not a drop of rain or snow would touch the Imperial family as they boarded and alighted. The grand Imperial reception rooms, built for the sole use of the Czar and his entourage, are now the main exhibition area of the National Railway Museum, displaying model steam engines, uniforms and railway documents and posters.
Raudtee 2. Tel: (372) 473 7165. www.jaam.ee. Open: Wed–Sun 10am–6pm. Admission charge.

HAAPSALU ENVIRONS

Haapsalu is a good base for a visit to one of Estonia's largest areas of natural beauty, and for a trip to nearby islands.

Matsalu National Park

Matsalu is the western mainland's most important nature reserve and embraces the shoreline and shallow waters of Matsalu Bay, which are ideal for wading birds and waterfowl. In the bay, the reserve also comprises more than 50 islands close to the shore where numerous birds nest, and huge reedbeds provide shelter for still more rare bird species. Inland lie the flood plains of the Kasari, Raana and Roude rivers, coastal meadows that attract huge numbers of ducks and geese, and

THE WHITE LADY OF HAAPSALU CASTLE

During the Middle Ages, this castle was the seat of an order of celibate warrior-priests. Women were banned from its precincts. The White Lady, who is said to haunt the castle, is supposedly the ghost of a young woman who had an affair with one of the priests, disguising herself as a pageboy to visit her lover. When found out, she was punished by being impaled on the castle walls. Her ghost is claimed to appear in one of the castle windows on August nights.

Matsalu Nature Reserve is ideal for birdwatching

wooded meadows that create a unique environment for many wild flowers, butterflies and amphibians. In all, 275 bird species, 49 kinds of fish and 47 mammal species are registered in the park area. Guided tours on foot or by boat can be arranged with the park headquarters, near Lihula, and there are birdwatching hides and towers near Haeska, on the north side of the bay, and Matsalu village on the south side of the bay.

Matsalu Nature Reserve Visitor Centre, Penijoe Manor, 3km (2 miles) north of Lihula. Open: mid-Apr–mid-Sept Wed, Thur, Sat & Sun 8am–5pm, Fri 8am–3.45pm. Tel: (372) 472 4236. www.matsalu.ee. Admission free.

Vormsi

The little island of Vormsi is just 20km (12 miles) long and lies only a few kilometres from the western mainland, from which it is separated by the Voosi channel. For centuries, this peaceful, wooded isle was a Swedish enclave, but most of its 2,000-strong population fled to Sweden in 1944 to escape the advancing Red Army, leaving only an array of Swedish-sounding place names as evidence of their presence. Vormsi's thick woods shelter deer, wild boar and elk, and many sea birds roost around its shores. Boats from Rohuküla, on the mainland 8km (5 miles) west of Haapsalu, anchor at Sviby on the south coast of Vormsi. The small island capital, Hullo, is a quiet village of old-fashioned buildings. Nearby, St Olav's Church is testimony to the island's Scandinavian heritage. Dating from 1929, it stands on the site of a 13th-century church.

Vormsi is 6km (4 miles) north of Haapsalu. Ferries from Rohuküla.

Hiiumaa

Although it is Estonia's second-largest island (after Saaremaa), Hiiumaa is surprisingly empty and offers only basic services for visitors, with a few simple guesthouses and places to eat. Much of the island is covered by

In winter Vormsi is covered in layers of snow

Manor house at Lihula

juniper and pine trees and peat marsh, and Hiiumaa is an ideal getaway for nature-lovers. The main village, Kärdla, is on the island's north coast, but ferries from the mainland arrive at Heltermaa, near the southeast tip of the island. Hiiumaa's attractions are natural rather than man-made. Kassari village, however, on a smaller island just off the south coast of Hiiumaa, linked to it by a road causeway, is an attractive jumble of old-fashioned wooden houses surrounding a unique thatched church. It has a small museum with a collection of old farm tools and island costumes.

Kõpu Lighthouse

This 15th-century lighthouse is Hiiumaa's best-known landmark, and perches on the highest point of the island, 5km (3 miles) inland. Erected in 1490, it remained in use until 1997, and was refurbished in 2002. From the top of the 100m (328ft) tower, it is possible to see as far as Saaremaa, 50km (31 miles) south of Kärdla.
Bus from Kärdla. Open: daily 9am–sunset. Admission charge.

Soera Farm Museum

The buildings of this delightful open-air museum have been preserved exactly as they were in the mid-19th century. Many of the farm implements and household utensils are original, including a wooden spinning wheel and handloom from the days when islanders had to spin and weave their own cloth. The museum also has its own restaurant and brewery.
Bus from Kärdla to Palade.
Palade village, 8km (5 miles) southeast of Kärdla. Tel: (372) 566 6895. www.hiumaa.ee. Open: mid-May–Aug noon–6pm; Sept noon–4pm. Closed: rest of the year. Admission charge.

Lihula

The little farming town of Lihula, which is a few kilometres inland from Matsalu Bay, is the best base for exploring the Matsalu Nature Reserve and a handy place to stop on the way to Muhu and Saaremaa. It lies 120km (75 miles) southwest of Tallinn.
Buses from Tallinn and Virtsu.

Migrant birds

Estonia's many wetland and coastal nature reserves attract huge numbers of migrant geese, ducks and other waterfowl, including several rare and endangered species that are hard to see anywhere else in Europe. Estonia's islands and forests also provide shelter for migrant birds on their journey between their summer feeding and nesting grounds in Scandinavia and the Arctic, and their winter homes in southern Europe and North Africa.

Some Arctic birds come south to Estonia's relatively mild climate for the winter, heading north again in spring.

A mute swan on the Baltic Sea

Ornithologists estimate that more than one million birds of up to 40 different species pass through Estonia each year. Spring and autumn are the best times to visit the country's wildlife reserves. Bird species include barnacle geese and greylag geese, ducks such as teal, scoter and gadwall, Bewick's swans, and raptors including the white-tailed eagle.

Among the most spectacular migrant visitors to Estonia's wetlands, however, are the cranes and black storks which can sometimes be seen in such numbers that they darken the sky as they fly. Around 30,000 common cranes rest in Estonia's meadows and marshes on their annual migrations, and many nest in the wetlands and peat bogs of western Estonia.

Visitors can volunteer to help with counting the cranes at Matsalu Bay in Matsalu National Park in western Estonia every autumn in the third week in September, when up to 10,000 of these birds visit the park. The west coast of Saaremaa, Käina Bay and the many small islands around Hiiumaa are also superb birdwatching territory.

Ironically, the strict military regulations of the era of the Soviet

Common crane

occupation, which placed much of Estonia's coasts and forests off-limits to hunters, foresters and farmers, created safe havens for many of Europe's rarest birds. The black stork, which nests only in undisturbed forests where the trees may be up to two centuries old, finds expanses of such forests in the Estonian hinterland.

Estonia's untouched woodlands also shelter resident species such as the endangered white-backed woodpecker, three-toed woodpecker and black woodpecker.

These deep forests are also the perfect habitat for some of Europe's most spectacular diurnal and nocturnal raptors, including the lesser-spotted eagle, the golden eagle and the spectacular, but rarely seen, eagle owl.

The magnificent golden eagle

Global climate change is already changing the migratory patterns of many of the birds that make landfall in Estonia each year – some experts think the presence of the white stork shows that global warming may have begun much earlier than the 21st century.

The first white storks appeared in Estonia in the 1830s, and began nesting here as long ago as 1841 – evidence that Estonia and northern Europe may already have begun to grow warmer more than 150 years ago. More than 2,000 pairs of these graceful birds now nest in Estonia every summer, making untidy nests in trees, on disused chimneys and man-made nesting platforms.

PÄRNU

Pärnu, on the shores of the Gulf of Rīga and at the mouth of the Pärnu River, is Estonia's lively, stylish summer capital. Its sandy beaches, yacht marina, thermal spas and pretty surroundings attract large numbers of summer visitors from Tallinn and other parts of Estonia, as well as from Russia and the other Baltic republics. In fact, Pärnu's population of 50,000 rises to more than 150,000 during the peak holiday season.

Surprisingly, few Western visitors have discovered its charms, which include a thriving cultural scene, an array of summer music festivals, and arguably the country's liveliest nightlife. Several of Tallinn's major dance and rock music venues relocate to Pärnu for the holiday season in July and August. The town's 8km (5-mile) sandy beach is arguably the best in Estonia, with shallow water that becomes pleasantly warm in high summer. Within easy reach of Pärnu are the natural beauty and wildlife of the Soomaa National Park and the pretty island of Kihnu, in the Gulf of Rīga. With numerous comfortable places to stay and some of the country's best places to eat and drink, it is only a matter of time before Pärnu becomes a much more popular destination for foreign visitors. Much of Pärnu is relatively modern, at least by Estonian standards. It was founded by merchants of the Hanseatic League in 1346. During the Middle Ages, it became an important seaport. Very little remains, however, of the medieval town, apart from the Red Tower at the corner of Hospidali and Uus streets, which was part of the 15th-century fortifications, and the 17th-century Tallinn Gate, at the west end of Louna. This gate led through the old city walls. Pärnu's grid-style street plan and many of its public buildings and stylish private villas date from the 19th century, when commerce gave way to leisure as the country's main source of prosperity. Sea-bathing establishments began to open in the mid-19th century, the yacht club opened in 1906, and by the eve of World War II, the town attracted almost 7,000 summer visitors each year, many of whom stayed at luxurious establishments such as the

The Red Tower

Bristol Hotel, built in 1900. It is still a Pärnu landmark. Other city landmarks include the Town Hall, a classical building erected in 1797. St Catherine's Church, which faces the Town Hall, was completed in 1768 and named in honour of the Russian Czarina, Catherine the Great. With its ornate domes and spires, it is one of Estonia's finest baroque buildings, and its interior boasts a plethora of gorgeously coloured Orthodox icons in costly gilt and silver frames. Dating from a slightly earlier era, St Elizabeth's Church, at the corner of Kuninga and Nikolai streets, was completed in 1747. It too is named after a Russian empress. The city's newest and most prominent landmark, however, is the striking modern Concert Hall, on Aida. This stunning glass auditorium opened in 2002, at a cost of almost 6 million euros, and has become one of Estonia's most important venues for classical music and opera performances. Pärnu can also claim to be Estonia's most important centre for the visual arts, with several galleries which display the work of some of the country's cutting-edge contemporary artists.

Pärnu's centre is compact and pedestrian-friendly and the best way to explore all its sights is on foot.

140km (87 miles) south of Tallinn.

City Art Gallery

The City Art Gallery is housed within the new Pärnu Concert Hall complex and provides an appropriately modern

St Elizabeth's Church

space for exhibitions by living Estonian painters, sculptors and printmakers. *Aida 4. Open: Tue–Fri noon–7pm, Sat noon–5pm. Admission charge.*

Lydia Koidula Memorial Museum

This interesting museum is housed in a 19th-century former schoolhouse and was opened in 1945. It commemorates the life and work of Lydia Koidula (1843–86), the Estonian poet who spent most of her life in Pärnu, and who was one of the guiding spirits of Estonia's 19th-century cultural renaissance. She was among the first to write lyric poetry in the Estonian language. The

St Catherine's Church

Pärnu beach

collection illustrates her career and that of her father, Johann Voldemar Lannsen, who founded the country's first Estonian-language newspaper and was also a leading campaigner in the 19th-century drive to forge an Estonian national identity.
J V Jansenni 37. Tel: (372) 443 3313. www.pernau.ee. Open: Wed–Sun 10am–6pm. Admission charge.

Pärnu City Museum

Pärnu's city museum houses one of Estonia's largest collections of archaeological discoveries, including Neolithic finds from an 11,000-year-old settlement unearthed at Sindi.
Aida 4. Tel: (372) 443 3231. www.pernau.ee. Open: Tue–Sat 10am–6pm. Admission charge.

Pärnu Contemporary Art Museum

Also called the Chaplin Centre (although it has no real links with Charlie Chaplin), this art gallery is in the forefront of Estonian new art, with a permanent exhibition of work by 20th- and 21st-century artists along with a programme of temporary exhibitions. The centre opened in 1992. Since then its exhibition has expanded to include more than 1,000 works. Not all are brilliant (it seems that the curators value novelty and shock value more highly than conventional artistic merit), but the exhibits are always interesting and sometimes provocative.
Esplanaadi 10. Tel: (372) 443 0772. www.chaplin.ee. Open: daily 9am–9pm. Admission charge.

PÄRNU ENVIRONS

There is plenty to keep the visitor busy in Pärnu for several days (and nights), but the surrounding coastline, offshore islands and countryside are also well worth exploring by car, by bicycle or by bus.

Beaches

Pärnu's beaches, with long stretches of fine white sand, are probably the best, and certainly the busiest, in Estonia. They begin on the southwest side of town, where the Art Deco Pärnu Mud Baths offer a variety of supposedly health-enhancing treatments, and extend for several kilometres southward along the shore of Pärnu bay.

A lifeguard tower on Pärnu beach

Estonian Museum Railway

This museum is the third-largest in Europe, with a working collection of narrow-gauge locomotives and rolling stock, and 2km (1¼ miles) of track along which the old-fashioned trains run hourly trips on Saturdays. Since 2005, there have been plans to relocate the Museum Railway to Türi (*see p91*), so before making a special excursion it is advisable to check the museum's website (*see below*). Museum trains operate on Saturdays only.

Bus 44 from Pärnu. Lavassaare, 15km (9 miles) northwest of Pärnu. Tel: (372) 527 2584. www.museumrailway.ee. Open: 6 June–30 Sept Wed–Sat 11am–6pm, Sun 10–3pm.

Häädemeeste

Häädemeeste, on the coast midway between Pärnu and the Latvian border, is a quiet village which was founded by Estonian shipowners, many of whose imposing 19th-century mansions may still be seen. It has a small museum with an eclectic collection of household items from the 1920s and 1930s, and to the north of the village are the Rannametsa sand dunes, an area of deserted sandy beaches and remarkable natural beauty. Just inland from the dunes (across Highway 4, which runs parallel to the coast between Pärnu and the Latvian border) is the Soometsa-Rannametsa Regional Nature Reserve, an area of sandy heath, dunes and peat marsh notable for coastal plants and numerous butterfly species.

Old-fashioned trains at the Estonian Museum Railway

Buses from Pärnu run approximately hourly. Buses from Häädemeeste continue south to Ikla, on the Latvian border. 70km (43 miles) south of Pärnu. As of 2005, the border crossing was open only to Estonians and Latvians.

Kihnu

Kihnu island is the largest island within the Gulf of Rīga, but with an area of only 17sq km (6½sq miles), it is easy to explore the whole island on a short visit. Kihnu has a population of 600 people, most of them fisherfolk who preserve many of their island traditions. Kihnu's main attraction is its air of peaceful isolation.

It escaped both the ravages of World War II and the industrialisation of the Soviet era, so much of the island still looks much as it must have done during the first half of the 20th century. Its shores attract a number of sea-bird species, and its biggest landmark is its lighthouse, on the southern tip of the island, which was imported from Britain and erected in 1864.

Ferries twice daily. 41km (25 miles) southwest of Pärnu.

Nigula Nature Reserve

This reserve close to the Latvian border encloses an area of ponds and peat bogs that provides a breeding refuge for many rare birds. Much of the reserve is off-limits to casual visitors to avoid disturbing the breeding sites, but there is a waymarked 6.8km (4¼-mile) walking trail near the reserve headquarters at Vanajarve. The Estonian and Latvian governments have plans to expand the reserve across the border to protect a larger expanse of peat bog and plant, animal and bird habitats.

Buses from Pärnu and Viljandi. 70km (43 miles) south of Pärnu.

Windmills on Saaremaa

Soomaa National Park

It lies midway between Pärnu and Viljandi (*see p94*) and is as easy to reach from Pärnu as it is from Viljandi, and Kihnu island makes a pleasant day trip.

SAAREMAA AND MUHU

Saaremaa is Estonia's largest island, with a population of around 40,000 people. Its coastline is deeply indented, and hundreds of tiny, uninhabited islets lie close to its shores. Kuressaare, the island capital and the main port on Saaremaa, lies on the sheltered south coast. The smaller island of Muhu lies between Saaremaa and the mainland. Ferries connect Muhu with the mainland port of Virtsu, and a road bridge connects Muhu with its larger neighbour, so it makes sense to treat the two islands as a single destination. Saaremaa's landscapes are a mixture of gentle farmland, lakes and birch and conifer woods, surrounded by a rugged coastline and many smaller satellite islands. Saaremaa is also noted for its windmills. Some of the most picturesque of these can be seen at Angla (*60km/37 miles north of Kuressaare*).

Muhu is much smaller than Saaremaa. Ferries from the mainland arrive at its main port of Kuivastu, and the island has fewer attractions for the visitor than its neighbour, though its small museum is worth a visit. Also worth seeing is the remarkable church at Liiva, built during the 13th century, when the island was in the hands of the Teutonic Knights. It was extensively restored in 1994. Its mural paintings, dating from the 14th century, were covered over with plaster during the Protestant Reformation of the 16th century and were rediscovered only in 1913.

Ferries from Virtsu.

Kaali Crater Field and Visitor Centre

Saaremaa's most unusual natural feature is the 100m (328ft) wide circular lake formed by the impact of a meteorite that struck the island around 5500 BC. The lake is surrounded by smaller impact craters and is believed to have been a worship site for the pagan people of pre-Christian Estonia, and various legends seek to explain how the craters were created. The visitor centre contains samples of meteoric rock and a display on the history and geology of the area.

Kaali Visitor Centre, Kaali village (3km/2 miles north of the Kuivaste–Kuressaare highway, 18km/11 miles east of Kuressaare, signposted). Tel: (372) 514 4889.

Kuressaare

Kuressaare is the prettiest of Estonia's island towns, with a charming mixture of neoclassical, northern Gothic and baroque architecture that harks back to its heyday as a 1930s health and holiday resort. It reflects Saaremaa's chaotic history. The Teutonic Knights conquered the island in 1227 and ruled it until 1557, when they were evicted by the Danes. Over the next century the island repeatedly changed hands between Denmark, Sweden and Russia

The meteorite crater at Kaali

The lighthouse in Vilsandi National Park

until – along with the rest of the Estonian islands – it finally fell to Peter the Great of Russia. Three large spa complexes, which have been built since independence from the Soviet Union, dominate the harbour area where a new cruise ship quay opened in 2007, but the rest of Kuressaare is pleasantly old-fashioned. The Town Hall was originally built in 1654 but was restored in the 1960s, and there are attractive stone-built town houses with red-tiled roofs along streets in the town centre, notably Kauba (off the Town Hall Square) and Tallinna. Kuressaare Castle, dating from 1340, was the seat of a medieval bishopric, and is one of the most imposing medieval strongholds in Estonia. Its thick stone walls and towers surround an inner courtyard. The castle houses the Saaremaa Museum, which was founded in 1865 and includes exhibits which illuminate the island's past up to modern times, including ecclesiastical vestments and medieval weaponry. Kuressaare is midway along the south coast of Saaremaa island. All sites can be visited on foot.

Kuressaare Castle, Lossihoov 1, Kuressaare. Tel: (372) 455 7542. Open: May–Aug Wed–Sun 10am–6pm; Sept–Apr Wed–Sun 11am–6pm. Admission charge.

Mihkli Farm Museum

The main attraction of this open-air museum is a working windmill, which is surrounded by a cluster of stone-walled cottages thatched with reeds, which grow plentifully around the island's shores.

Island bus from Kuressaare. Viki village, Saaremaa, 32km (20 miles) northwest of Kuressaare. Open: mid-Apr–Sept daily 10am–6pm. Admission charge.

Muhu Museum

This is a fascinating collection of old farm buildings, thatched cottages and a village school, all dating from the late 19th and early 20th centuries. The museum also has a colourful exhibition of traditional costumes and quilts.
Koguva village, Muhu island, 19km (12 miles) west of Kuivastu. Tel: (372) 454 8885. www.muhumuuseum.ee. Open: May–Aug Wed–Sun 10am–6pm; Sept–Apr Wed–Sun 11am–6pm. Admission charge.

Vilsandi National Park

The Vilsandi National Park comprises around 160 rocky islets, bays and peninsulas on Saaremaa's west coast and has been designated a reserve to protect some 500 plant species and almost 250 kinds of sea bird and waterfowl, including huge flocks of eider duck, gulls, terns, cormorants, barnacle geese and other migrants and resident birds. As many as one million birds migrate through the region on their way between their breeding areas in the Arctic region and their winter refuges in southern Europe and Africa.
Bus from Kuressaare to Kihelkonna village. West coast of Saaremaa, 30km (19 miles) west of Kuressaare.
Arrange visits with park headquarters at Loona village (tel: (372) 454 6704; open: Mon–Fri 9am–5pm).
Park open: daily, at any time. Admission free.

A thatched cottage at Muhu Museum

Walk: Pärnu

Pärnu is the most pleasant of all Estonian towns to explore on foot. It offers green spaces, historic buildings – most of them dating from the 18th and 19th century – a long stretch of beach that is perfect for a summer swim, and lots of cafés and bars to pause at along the way. Allow three hours to complete this walk at a leisurely pace, and in summer plan to finish it with a swim at one of Estonia's best beaches.

Distance: 3km (2 miles).

Start at Town Hall Square (Raekoja plats), dominated by the elegantly strict classical façade of the Town Hall.

1 Town Hall

Originally the private dwelling of a wealthy merchant, it was built in 1797 and became the municipal seat in 1839.

Leave the square from its northwest corner, turning left, and walk less than 50m (55yds) to St Catherine's Church, at Vee 16.

Neoclassical Pärnu Mud Baths

2 St Catherine's Church

St Catherine's is the most richly adorned baroque church in Estonia, and was built in 1768 on the site of an earlier wooden church. With its emerald-green domes and spire, it is an unmissable landmark.

Carry on down Vee and turn right (west) at the corner of Vee and Kuninga, then walk to the end of Kuninga.

3 The Tallinn Gate

The Tallinn Gate is one of the few surviving features of Pärnu's ring of medieval fortifications. From here, a ferry crossed the Pärnu River to connect with the old highway to Tallinn. The elegant arched gateway, finished in pale blue and white stucco, was restored in 1980.

Leaving the Tallinn Gate, head south on Remmelga, and after one block, turn left (east) onto Esplanaadi. Follow this avenue for two blocks to the corner of Esplanaadi and Supeluse, and the Pärnu Contemporary Art Museum.

4 Pärnu Contemporary Art Museum

This gallery has a permanent collection of work by 20th- and 21st-century artists, as well as temporary exhibitions.

Turn right on Supeluse and walk south, towards the mud baths at Ranna 1.

5 Pärnu Mud Baths

Carefully laid-out gardens surround the elegant neoclassical portico and domed roof of the Pärnu Mud Baths. Mineral-rich mud from the Pärnu region is credited with curative properties for a variety of ailments, including arthritis and rheumatism.

Pärnu beach is within sight, less than 50m (55yds) south of the Mud Baths.

6 Pärnu beach

The parts of the beach closest to town are the most crowded, but also have the best choice of beach cafés and bars for a post-swim drink and snack.

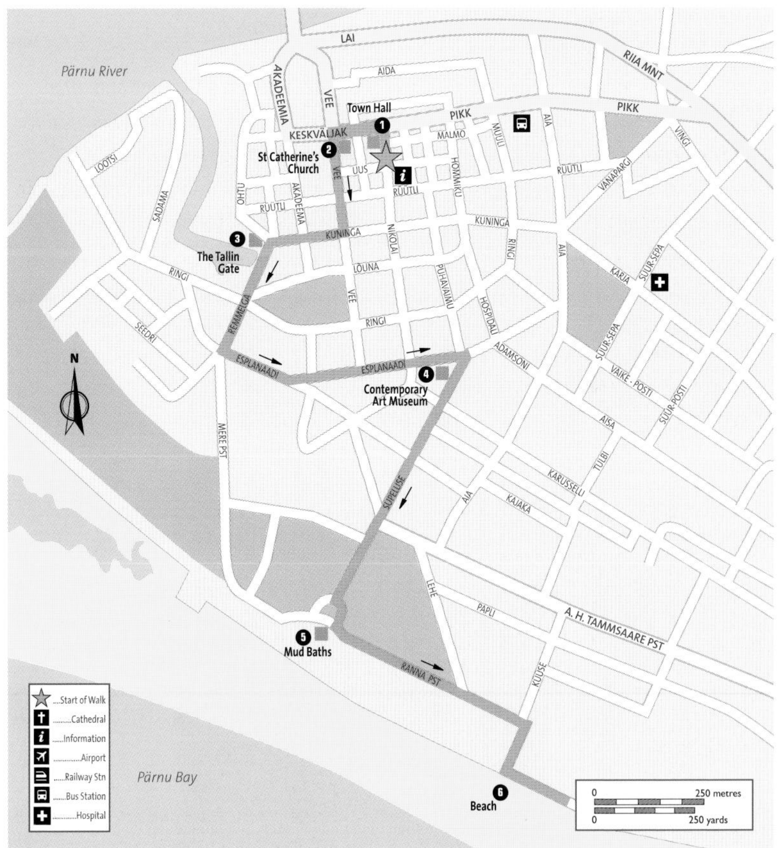

Drive: Around Saaremaa Island

Estonia's biggest island is full of surprises. Saaremaa is a place of varied landscapes, from rolling farmland and woodland to rugged shores and offshore islets. Rich in wildlife, Saaremaa is also rich in history, with little medieval churches, small villages and picturesque windmills, and its north coast looks out across the Baltic to its northern neighbour, Hiiumaa.

Distance: 150km (93 miles).

Time: A full day (around 10 hours).

Leave Kuressaare on route 74, heading northeast. After 26km (16 miles), turn left (north) to route 79. Pass through Liiva-Putla village and after 2km (1¼ miles) turn right to the Kaali Crater, clearly signposted.

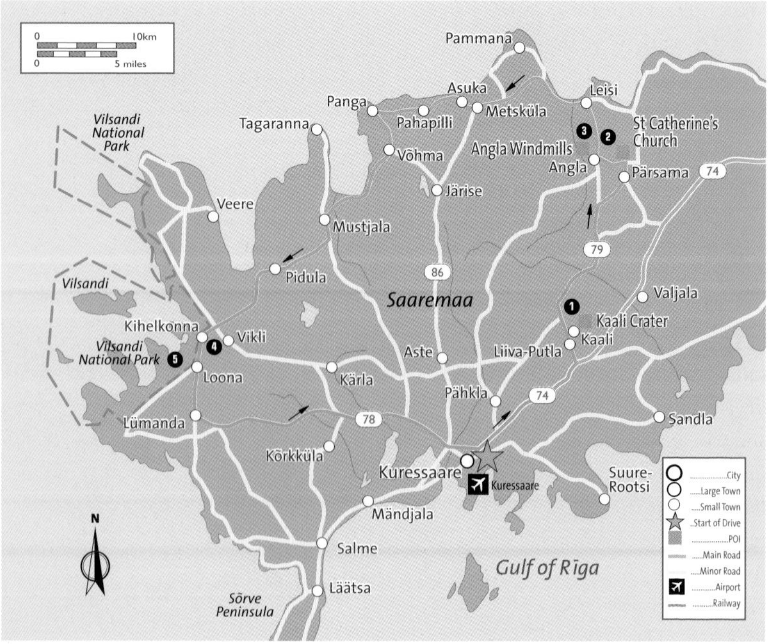

1 Kaali Crater

The crater, formed by the impact of a meteor around 5500 BC, is one of Estonia's strangest natural sights. The jade-green pool, nearly 100m (110yds) across, is an almost perfect circle and was a sacred site to pre-Christian Estonians.

Return to the main road and continue north on route 79. After 17km (11 miles), turn right to Pärsama village and St Catherine's Church, just north of the village centre.

2 St Catherine's Church

St Catherine's, the 15th-century church of Karja parish, is the smallest place of worship on Saaremaa and one of the prettiest. Its wall frescoes show pagan influences, and its carved roof-pillars were the work of masons from all over the Baltic region.

Leaving Pärsama, follow the road as it curves northwest to arrive after 2km (1¼ miles) at Angla.

3 Angla Windmills

Saaremaa once boasted hundreds of windmills, and tourist maps still show lots of windmill symbols, but the five square towers that stand here are among the last that survive in working order and have become symbolic of the island.

Rejoining route 79, drive north to Leisi, then turn left (west) on an unsurfaced road through Meiuste and Metsküla to Asuka. Drive 5km (3 miles) further west to Panga. Just north of the village is a car park and a viewpoint with a spectacular panorama of Saaremaa's north coast. From Panga, follow the main route 86 for 4km (2½ miles) to Võhma and turn right to Mustjala. At Mustjala, turn left, then after 1km (⅔ mile) turn right through the tiny village of Pidula and continue to Kihelkonna.

4 Kihelkonna

Kihelkonna is the largest village in southwest Saaremaa, with a picturesque 13th-century church. Just south of the village, at Vikli, the Mihkli Farm Museum is also worth a short detour.

Drive southwest for 5km (3 miles) to Loona and the headquarters of the Vilsandi National Park.

5 Vilsandi National Park

The park encloses an expanse of narrow bays, tiny islands and rocky headlands and provides a refuge for thousands of sea birds and waterfowl. There are several observation towers, and guided tours can be arranged from the park headquarters.

From Vilsandi, return to Kihelkonna and follow route 78 for 32km (20 miles) back to Kuressaare.

Saaremaa Island

Walk: Kuressaare

To stroll through Kuressaare's streets is to take a walk through Estonia's history. The wars that ravaged the mainland over several centuries left this island capital almost untouched, as did Soviet-era industrialisation, and Kuressaare has a surprising heritage of baroque, northern Gothic and neoclassical architecture. With only 16,000 inhabitants, Kuressaare is a small town, and this is a short walk.

Distance: 1.8 km (1 mile). Time: 90 minutes including visit to castle museums and shops.

Start your walk at the entrance to the castle, at the south end of Lossi, and walk south to the castle entrance.

1 Kuressaare Episcopal Castle

This no-nonsense castle is the best-preserved medieval fortress in Estonia. The earliest part of the castle dates from the mid-14th century, and the impressive outer earthworks were added a century later. It was occupied successively by Danes, Germans, Swedes and Russians, and its last garrison left in 1836. Since 1865 the inner castle has housed the Saaremaa Museum, with a permanent collection of old weapons and costumes.

Kuressaare Castle with moat

Carry on across the castle lawns, cross the south moat and turn right on Kalda pst to Pargi.

2 Suur Toll and Piret

Where Kalda and Pargi meet, a cartoonish statue by Tauno Kungro (2002) is of Suur Toll (Toll the Great), the legendary king of Saaremaa, and his wife Piret.

Follow Pargi clockwise round the park to return to Lossi, and walk north up Lossi to the junction with A. Kitzbergi.

3 St Nicholas Church

Built in 1790, this Orthodox church looks exotic, with its copper domes and spire. At present the church is closed for restoration; by 2008, this work should have been completed.

Continue north on Lossi for 350m (380yds) to the corner of Kauba and Lossi. On your left is a small public garden; in the centre of this is the Independence Monument.

4 Independence Monument

Built in 1928, this statue – of a stricken but still defiant Estonian soldier – commemorates the islanders who died in Estonia's first independence war.

Past the monument, continue north to Raekoja plats (Town Hall Square).

5 Raekoja plats (Town Hall Square)

On the east side of the square the Town Hall, built in 1670, retains the stone lions which guarded an earlier town hall, and its ground floor now houses the local tourist office. Opposite the town hall, the Weigh House (now a café-bar) was built in 1666. It originally housed the public scales used to present traders from giving short measures.

Continue northeast to St Lawrence Church.

6 St Lawrence Church

This church was originally built in the 17th century but was destroyed by fire. Since then it has been rebuilt several times.

For a drink or a snack, walk back to Raekoja plats.

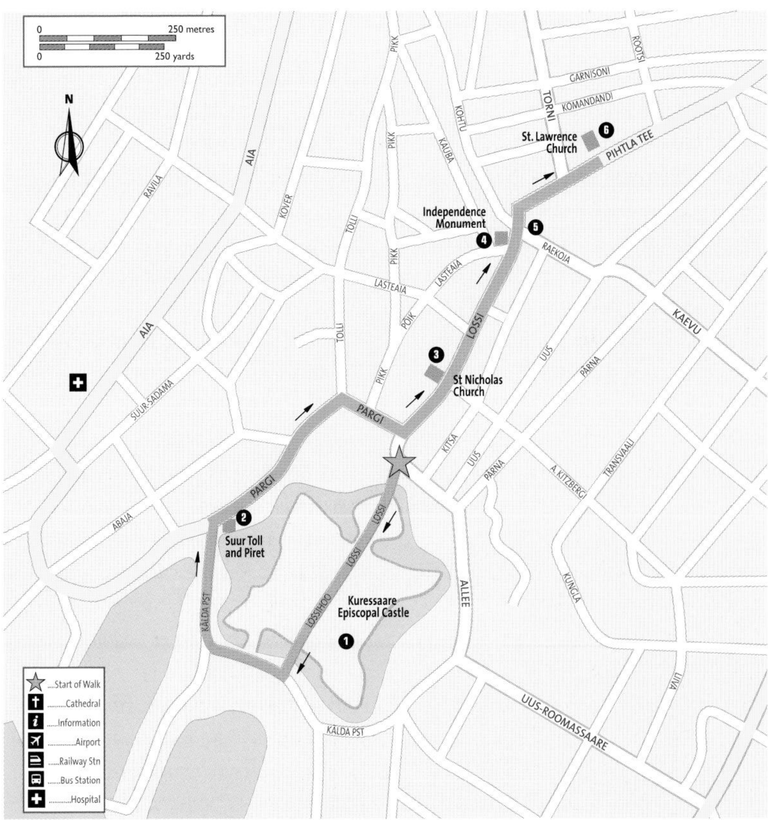

Walk: Haapsalu

This seaside stroll takes you through an Estonian seaside town that has only just begun to emerge from its Soviet-era time capsule and that exhibits a quirky charm, with mementoes of its heyday as a playground for the cream of 19th-century Imperial Russia. In summer, you can wind up with a swim.

Distance: 2.5–3km (1½–2 miles).

Time: 3 hours, including visits to the sights, and add on an hour or more if you want to spend time on the beach.

Start this walk at the castle, in the centre of Haapsalu on Lossi plats.

1 Haapsalu Castle

The forbidding ramparts of the 13th-century bishop's castle, now a picturesque, part-ruined landmark, dominate the town centre. The outer walls, almost 1km (⅔ mile) long, enclose the combined castle and cathedral, part of which now houses a museum with a collection of medieval weapons. To get an overview of the rest of Haapsalu, climb the castle watchtower.

From the castle grounds, turn north (left) on Vee and walk 100m (110yds) to the seashore. Turn left and follow the esplanade for less than 100m (110yds) to the Kurhaus.

2 Kurhaus

Built in 1898 as a venue for concerts and dances, the elegant Kurhaus and its bandstand have come back into their own since independence. Neglected during the Soviet period, it was reopened as an open-air café in 1997.

From the Kurhaus, follow the Promenaadi north, passing some elegant 19th-century villas and hotels, to the grand Hotel Promenaadi, formerly an aristocratic residence.

3 Tchaikovsky Bench

In front of the Hotel Promenaadi, the Tsaikovsky Pink (Tchaikovsky Bench) is a memorial to the Russian composer, who visited Haapsalu in 1867 and wrote several works here. It was built in 1940, but the excerpts from his works that are played automatically as you approach are a more modern touch.

Continue north on Promenaadi for around 200m (220yds) to the Rannarootsi Museum at Sadama 32.

4 Rannarootsi Museum (Museum of the Estonian Swedes)

Many of Haapsalu's families claim Swedish descent, although most Estonian

Swedes fled to Sweden during and after World War II. The museum displays colourful traditional costumes and a lively tapestry, made in 2002, that tells the tale of the Swedes in Estonia from Viking times to the 20th century.

The next stop is around 1.6km (1 mile) south. You can either walk south, along the west side of the Väike-Viik lagoon, and follow Kaida on down to the station, or alternatively you can take a taxi to the station from the Hotel Promenaadi.

5 Estonian Railway Museum

No longer in use, the 19th-century railway station, which was built for the convenience of the Russian Imperial family and their retinue on their visits to Haapsalu, is now a museum with models of steam trains, old railway uniforms, posters and documents.

On a fine day, you can finish this walk with a swim or a beach picnic. Cross the railway by walking west on Jaama after leaving the station, to reach the long, sandy Paralepa Beach.

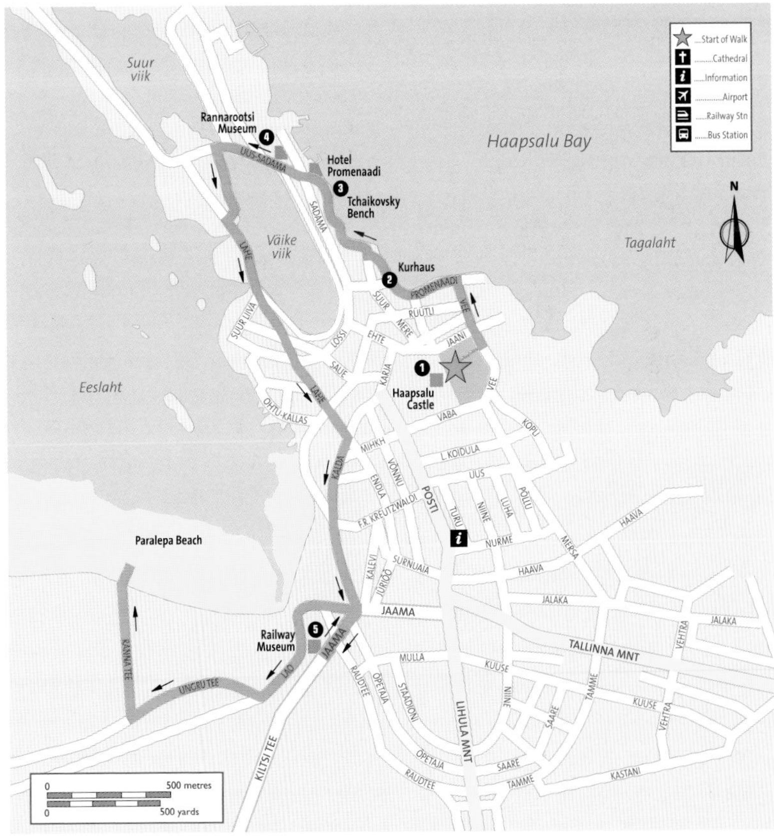

Drive: Around Hiiumaa Island

Estonia's second-largest island is a peaceful place that receives surprisingly few visitors. In many ways this is Estonia in miniature, with sweeping views of the Baltic Sea, nature reserves and old-fashioned villages.

Distance: around 100km (62 miles).

Time: one day.

Start at Heltermaa, Hiiumaa's ferry port, and drive around the island anti-clockwise on route 80 for 19km (12 miles) to Palade village. The Soera Farm Museum is less than 1km (2/3 mile) further on, on your right.

1 Soera Farm Museum

This charming museum re-creates life on Hiiumaa around 150 years ago, with old wooden buildings, farm tools, household utensils and equipment including working spinning wheels and weaving looms. It even has its own brewery, as most large Estonian farms had in the mid-19th century.

Continue for 8km (5 miles) west to Kärdla, the island capital.

2 Kärdla

With its many wooden houses – most of which were built in the 1880s to house workers in the large weaving mill which was the town's biggest source of employment – Kärdla is quiet and surprisingly pretty. The former textile factory, Pikk Maja, on the main square, is now a local history museum and art gallery.

From Kärdla, drive 10km (6 miles) west on route 80, then turn right (north) on the unsurfaced road to Tahkuna and its landmark lighthouse.

3 Tahkuna Lighthouse

Built in 1875, the cast-iron lighthouse was designed in France and brought here in kit form to be assembled on the northernmost point of the island. Even more impressive than the lighthouse are the sea views. The bell that stands beside the lighthouse is a memorial to those who drowned when the ferry *Estonia* sank off Hiiumaa in 1994.

From Tahkuna you must backtrack to route 80 and continue westward to Kõrgessaare. This was once the largest village on the island but is now a dilapidated backwater. Carry on, on route 80, to Luidja village and follow the poorly surfaced road for around 10km (6 miles), to Kõpu.

4 Kõpu Nature Trail

The Kõpu Nature Trail begins 2km (1¼ miles) east of Kõpu village and is clearly signposted. It is an undemanding 2km (1¼-mile) hike, leading to a viewpoint 63m (207ft) above sea level. Many flower, plant and butterfly species can be seen in summer.

5 Kõpu Lighthouse

Estonia's oldest lighthouse dates from 1490, when it was erected to guide the merchant ships of the Hanseatic League. It remained in use for more than 500 years, and was renovated in 2002. Its viewing platform, 100m (328ft) above sea level, has superb panoramic views of Hiiumaa and neighbouring islands.

A further 10km (6 miles) of gravel road leads to the northwest tip of the island. Return to Kõpu village, then continue 8km (5 miles) to route 84 and turn right. Follow route 84 for 31km (19 miles) south to Emmaste.

6 Emmaste Church

Emmaste Church is famous for its 200kg (440lb) bronze bell, which villagers concealed from German looters and Soviet occupiers until after independence, when it was restored to its rightful place in the church tower, where it has become a symbol of newborn independence.

Follow route 83 northeast for around 40km (25 miles) to return to Heltermaa and the ferry to the mainland.

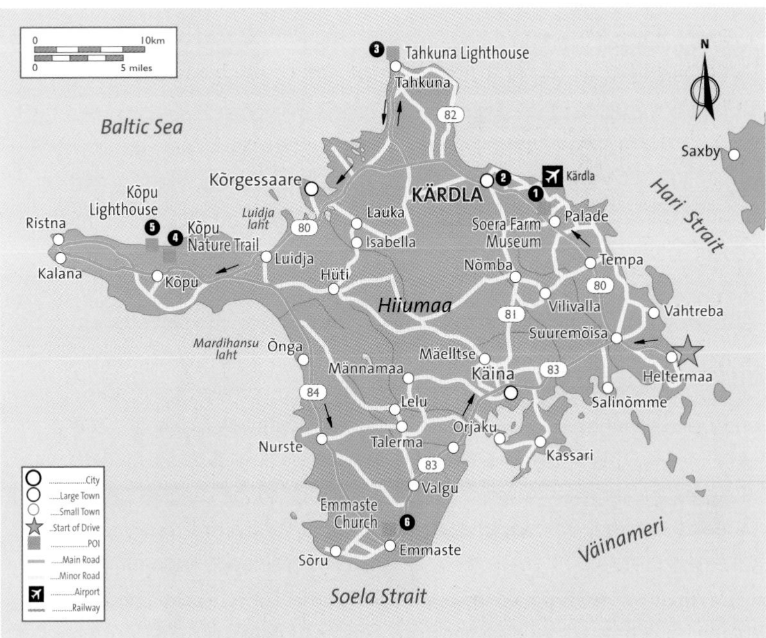

The Knights of the Sword

Founded in 1202 by Albert von Buxhoevden, Bishop of Rīga, the *Schwertbruderorden* (Order of the Brothers of the Sword), in their white cloaks bearing red crosses and swords, were sworn to conquer the region known as Livonia for the Christian Church. These warrior-monks were effective warriors, despite their Christian vows, and by 1227 (after making an uneasy alliance with Denmark) they controlled all of Estonia and its islands. Their methods were ruthless and brutal, even by the standards of medieval Europe, and by 1237, after being rebuked by the Pope for their treatment of their new and more disciplined Estonian subjects, the Brothers of the Sword were merged with the more disciplined Teutonic Order, becoming known as the Livonian Order. Five years later, the seemingly relentless eastward march of the Knights brought them into conflict with the powerful Slavic state of Novgorod, and their expansion was brought to an end when they were defeated, in 1242, by the Prince of Novgorod, in a battle fought on the frozen waters of Lake Peipsi.

The Knights eventually controlled the entire Estonian coastline, much of its hinterland, and the offshore islands, and reorganised the lands they had conquered into a loose federation of bishoprics, free cities such as Tallinn and Tartu, and knightly domains.

By 1346, this federation of barons and bishops was part of a strong feudal state, dominated by the Teutonic Knights from their grand master's headquarters at Marienburg (now Malbork in modern Poland) and stretching from the Estonian coast through Latvia to eastern Germany and parts of modern Poland.

The Knights and their vassals grew into the dominant power in Estonia and the neighbouring Baltic regions. Their estates grew prosperous by exporting grain to Germany and Scandinavia, and their armed might protected the trading posts, trade routes and merchant cities of the Hanseatic League within their domains. But further eastward expansion was blocked by the growing power of Muscovy and Novgorod. The Teutonic Order turned its efforts to the conquest and Christianisation of Lithuania. This proved their undoing in the end. Lithuania converted to Christianity under its own rulers in 1387, and in

Livonian Brothers of the Sword pay homage to Polish king Sigismundus Augustus

1410 the Knights suffered another decisive defeat at the bloody ten-hour battle of Grunwald (also known as Tannenberg) when the Grand Master of the Order was killed along with 205 of its knights.

From then on, it was downhill all the way for the Teutonic Order. After Grunwald, its knights were no longer a formidable military force, and the order gradually lost land and influence to the rising Baltic powers of Sweden, Poland-Lithuania and Russia. In 1525, the Order was formally dissolved by its last Grand Master, Frederick of Hohenzollern, and its lands were merged into a new hereditary Duchy of Prussia.
Frederick's descendants of the House of Hohenzollern went on to forge Prussia into a great European power, and ultimately to become rulers of a united German Empire that lasted until the end of World War I.
The descendants of the Livonian Knights continued to lord over their Estonian domains throughout the centuries of Swedish and Russian Imperial rule, and the castles and mansions that they constructed may be seen all over Estonia's mainland and islands.

Getting away from it all

Tallinn has established itself as one of the most popular destinations in Europe for a short city-break holiday, and surprisingly few foreign visitors see much of the rest of the country. Estonia, however, offers more than city nightlife and sightseeing. There are several spa resorts, offering therapeutic treatments using sea water and mineral mud. Vast areas of virtually virgin woodland and wetlands cover much of the hinterland, and large expanses of pristine wilderness are protected within nature reserves. Off the west coast, numerous islands, large and small, offer quiet getaways and untouched coastlines.

Canoeing

Canoeing on Estonia's lakes and waterways is a delightful way of getting away from it all, with fast-flowing rivers or quiet streams offering a variety of experiences for skilled or novice canoeists, ranging from half-day trips to longer floats lasting several days. Numerous companies offer guided canoeing trips, with river guides, meals, canoe rentals and safety equipment, all included in the price.

Cycling

Estonia is the perfect place for a cycling holiday. It is a small country, so cyclists can explore much of its hinterland in a one- or two-week holiday. Landscapes are remarkably varied, ranging from moorland and river valleys to thick forests and coastal cliffs, so travelling by bike is never boring. Most of the terrain is flat, and cycling is never hard work. Outside of the four major cities, motor traffic is relatively light. In summer,

The empty coast of Saaremaa Island is a great place to get away from it all

The ferry to Saaremaa

long hours of daylight mean cyclists can cover long distances, and there are plenty of campgrounds throughout the country, many of them offering accommodation in simple wooden cabins for those who do not wish to bring a tent. There is a large network of waymarked cycle routes, and numerous companies in Tallinn and elsewhere hire out bicycles (a list of such companies is available from tourist information offices). The Estonian Cycling Routes Network has been developed by national cycling clubs, the Estonian Tourist Board, the Estonian Environment Ministry and local authorities, and comprises national, regional and local routes. For a cycle route map, visit the website *www.visitestonia.com*

Island hopping

It is sometimes claimed that Estonia has several thousand offshore islands, but most are no more than uninhabited sandbanks or scraps of rock. Off the west coast and in the Gulf of Rīga, however, lies an archipelago of half a dozen inhabited islands, including Saaremaa (the largest), Hiiumaa, Vormsi, Muhu and Kihnu. Ruhnu, the most remote and most peaceful of these, is probably Estonia's ultimate getaway. It is located around 60km (37 miles) west of Ikla, on the Estonian coast. Getting there (and getting back to the mainland) is a challenge, as flights to Ruhnu from Pärnu operate only weekly and there is no regular ferry, but there is simple guesthouse accommodation on the island. The

Forest in Lahemaa National Park

larger isles are popular summer getaways for Estonians, and have frequent ferry connections to mainland ports and somewhat more sophisticated facilities for visitors.
(*See Western Estonia, pp104–9.*)

Nature reserves

Estonia is rich in natural beauty, and since independence from the Soviet Union in 1991, it has expanded the area of the country designated as nature reserves so that almost ten per cent of Estonia's total territory is now protected in one way or another, where a large number of birds, plants, insects, mammals, reptiles and amphibians find refuge. Even those who have no deep interest in wildlife will find these reserves the perfect antidote to the stresses of urban life. All the parks are open to the public, and most are free of charge. The more popular parks have waymarked walking trails, hides for birdwatchers, and also offer guided walks escorted by local wildlife experts. Estonia offers a much wider range of bird and mammal life than most of the rest of Europe. Its location between mainland Europe and the Arctic regions makes it fall on the path of many migratory birds, which rest in Estonia during their long migrations between their summer breeding grounds in the far north and their wintering areas in southern Europe and Africa. Estonia's thick forests also provide a home for large mammals including elk, wolf, deer, beaver, lynx and wild boar.

Alam-Pedja Nature Reserve, Haanja Natural Park

This nature park, 60km (37 miles) southeast of Tartu, surrounds Estonia's highest peak, Suur Munamägi (318m/1,043ft) and the country's deepest body of water, the 38m (125ft) deep Rouge Suurjarv lake.

Lahemaa National Park

This area of pine forests, sandy beaches and rocky headlands on the north coast is the easiest national park to get to from Tallinn, and can be visited on a day trip from the capital.

Matsalu National Park

Matsalu National Park is midway between Lihula and Haapsalu, also in Western Estonia. The offshore islands of Matsalu Bay, on the west coast, and the marshy plains inland from the coast, attract millions of migrant geese, ducks, divers, waders and other water birds which can be observed from birdwatching towers around the reserve.

Nigula Nature Reserve

About 45km (28 miles) south of Pärnu, this large expanse of peat marsh and almost 400 small lakes and pools is next to the Latvian border. There are plans to create a larger, cross-border reserve.

Soomaa National Park

Soomaa National Park is midway between Pärnu and Viljandi. It is a vast expanse of wetlands formed by four large peat mires, Kikepera, Kuresoo, Ordi and Valgeraba, and also by the water meadows of the Halliste River.

Vilsandi National Park

This lies 120km (75 miles) southwest of Tallinn, on the island of Saaremaa. It embraces a large area of coastline, hinterland, and more than 160 islets and rocky skerries, which shelter thousands of sea birds.

West coast of Saaremaa, 30km (19 miles) west of Kuressaare.

Matsalu National Park HQ and Museum

Sailing

Most Estonians were excluded from their own seas during the Soviet occupation, when the country's coastline was a high-security military area. Since independence, Estonians have enthusiastically reclaimed their sailing tradition, and there are yacht marinas at Pirita (just outside Tallinn) and at Toila, near Narva, where yachts can be chartered by the day or for longer trips along the coast or to the Estonian islands.

Trips to Finland

Less than two hours by high-speed hydrofoil from Tallinn, the Finnish capital Helsinki has long-standing links with Estonia. The Estonian and Finnish languages are very similar, and although Finland did not become a Soviet satellite state in the aftermath of World War II, it enjoyed a uniquely close relationship with the USSR. Finns travelled frequently to Tallinn even during the Soviet era. (*For details of ferry companies operating between Tallinn and Helsinki, see Practical Guide, p180.*)

Trips to Latvia

Estonia's southern neighbour shares a similar historical background, from conquest by Teutonic crusaders in the Middle Ages through to absorption into the Russian Empire, a brief flowering of independence between the two World Wars, incorporation into the Soviet Union, and eventual independence in 1991. That said, many visitors find Latvia a surprising contrast to Estonia. With a completely different language and a much larger and longer-established ethnic Russian population, Latvia is a very different country, with a more ambivalent relationship with the former USSR. While Estonians feel no nostalgia for the Soviet past, many older Latvians of Russian descent are less ready to consign those times to the dustbin of history. From Valga, in southern Estonia, it is possible to make a quick visit to the Latvian town of Valka as the two are really one conurbation, artificially separated by the border between the two countries, which is defined by a small stream, little more than a couple of metres wide. For a more in-depth experience of Latvia, it is easy to travel by rail or bus to Rīga, Latvia's capital, a journey of six to seven hours. Like Tallinn, Rīga has a restored medieval core surrounded by a post-war sprawl of Soviet-era factories and apartments, but the city centre is also graced by a wealth of elaborate and picturesque Jugendstil (Art Nouveau) buildings dating from the late 19th and early 20th centuries. Like Tallinn, Rīga has seen modern hotels, office blocks and department stores springing up in the city centre in the years since independence. The old quarter, Vecriga, is a clutter of medieval buildings between the Daugava River and the Pilsetas Canal. At the heart of the Old

An old fishing boat lies abandoned on Saaremaa

Town, the Romanesque Cathedral, dating from the early 13th century, is the city's most impressive relic of the Middle Ages, rivalled only by the Powder Tower, a sturdy 14th-century red-brick bastion with walls scarred by the artillery of several centuries of invading armies. Compared with the medieval strongholds of Estonia, Rīga Castle is something of a disappointment, as extensive rebuilding and alterations of several centuries have left nothing of its original towers and walls. The rather drab exterior of the castle conceals, however, three museums: the **Latvian History Museum**, the **Museum of Latvian Writing, Theatre and Music** and the **Foreign Art Museum**. St Peter's Church, with its distinctive triple spire, is Rīga's best-known landmark. Built during the 15th century, the main doorway of the red-brick medieval building is embellished by later baroque statuary. The gleaming steel spire is a 20th-century addition, replacing an 18th-century baroque steeple that was destroyed by German artillery fire in 1941.

(*For details of buses and trains between Rīga and Tallinn, see p179.*)

Hunting and ecotourism

Estonia's deep forests, which sheltered anti-Soviet partisans known as the 'Forest Brothers' during the Russian occupation, provide refuge for large wild animals that have been hunted to extinction in most of the rest of Europe.The largest populations of wolves, lynx and brown bear on the continent are found here.

Almost half of Estonia is covered with woodland, and the forests and their denizens hold a special place in the hearts of many Estonians. But there is also a strong tradition of hunting these wild predators, and hunters from other European countries and from America are willing to pay a substantial fee for a licence to hunt in Estonia. The State Forest Management Centre, which issues such licences, is responsible for 400,000ha (988,422 acres) of state-owned hunting reserves. The Centre estimates that Estonia has between 200 and 500 wolves, up to 900 lynx and around 600–800 brown bears. Hunting is a contentious topic, with traditionalists defending their right to shoot these animals, and an increasingly strong conservationist movement, which would like to see them more strongly protected.

Hunting was permitted under Soviet rule, but as large areas of

Lynx on the prowl

Roebucks with furry horns in springtime

forest fell within military zones, access was prohibited, and wild animals were unmolested. With independence, much more of Estonia's forest hinterland is open to hunters, and the country is freely accessible to large numbers of foreign sportsmen keen to bag an unusual trophy.

While there is little opposition to the shooting of elk, wild boar and deer, all of which are present in large numbers, even limited hunting of lynx, wolves and brown bear could threaten their existence in the future. All three species are either extinct or on the verge of extinction elsewhere in the European Union.

The shooting lobby counters opposition to hunting by claiming that properly limited hunting and well-managed game reserves actually benefit these animals, by keeping numbers down to manageable levels in areas set aside for them. There is a strong argument that the loss of habitat is a bigger threat to lynx, bear and wolf than shooting. The sale of hunting licences provides at least a cash incentive for the government to keep large areas of forests pristine, instead of allowing them to be opened up for logging, agriculture or industry.

However, there is an equally powerful claim that Estonia is uniquely suited to exploit the growing popularity of ecotourism. Canoeing, cycling, hiking and wildlife watching attract growing numbers of foreign visitors to Estonia's forests, and it may be that, as in African and Indian wildlife reserves, the photographer's telephoto lens will eventually become more popular than the hunter's rifle.

Shopping

Estonia joined the consumer world only recently. Compared to other holiday destinations, it offers relatively few exciting shopping opportunities or outstanding bargains. The choice of souvenirs is limited; there are few original locally made products of interest. Tallinn's shopping streets offer little that could not be bought in the UK, western Europe, or anywhere in the English-speaking world.

Hand-knitted sweaters, caps and scarves and traditional woven straw dolls and animal figures are among the better buys, along with hand-carved and lathe-turned wooden bowls, mugs and spoons. Amber jewellery (imported from neighbouring Latvia) is also popular.

Normal shopping hours are 10am–6pm on weekdays and 10am–5pm on Saturdays. Most shops (except those in Tallinn Old Town) close on Sundays. Larger department stores in Tallinn are generally open from 10am–8pm.

Major credit cards including Visa and MasterCard are accepted in larger shops, but cash is preferred in smaller establishments and in most shops outside the capital.

Antique collectors should be aware that items made before 1700 may not be exported, and a special permit is required to export items (including books) made in Estonia before 1945.

A souvenir shop in Tallinn

TALLINN

Tallinn's main western-style shopping streets are Viru and Muurihave, both in the Old Town and each with its share of stores selling clothes and accessories. The choice is not as wide as elsewhere in Europe, and prices are generally higher than in the UK or North America.

More typically Estonian buys can be found in the smaller stores in the lanes and courtyards of the Old Town, selling souvenirs, prints and paintings and local handicrafts and knitwear.

Lossi Plats

Watercolours, prints and oil paintings, mostly featuring stylised representations of the view of Old Tallinn from the top of Toompea, are sold by artists on the square in front of the castle and at the viewpoint platforms.
Summer daily 10am–9pm.

Masters' Courtyard

This quiet courtyard in the Old Town is dedicated to traditional arts, handicrafts and jewellery and is a good place to look for Baltic amber set in silver. Original prints and paintings are also sold here, as well as fine confectionery.
Vene 6, Tallinn. Tel: (372) 504 6113. Open: daily.

Muurihave Knitwear Market

Local craftswomen sell high-quality hand-knitted sweaters, scarves, hats, gloves and other knitwear from stalls along Muurihave, just inside the walls of the Old Town. The wool is fine and colours are generally muted, in tasteful shades of grey, blue, brown and green.
Muurihave, Old Town. Open: 9am–5pm.

St Catherine's Passage

Craft workshops line this small street in Tallinn's Old Town (near the Dominican Monastery) where visitors can watch potters, weavers, quiltmakers, embroiderers, glassblowers and silversmiths at work, as well as buy their finished products.
Between Vene and Muurihave, Tallinn. Open: daily except Sun.

Tallinna Kaubamaja

Tallinn's largest department store opened during the Soviet era but has moved on since then to offer a wide range of modern consumer goods. It is linked by a glass corridor to the newer Viru Centre (*see below*).
Gonsiori 2. Tel: (372) 667 3100. www.kaubamaja.ee

Viru Centre (Viru Keskus)

Tallinn's largest shopping mall has dozens of smarter stores, cafés and restaurants and is a popular local meeting place.
Viru väljak 4/6. Tel: (372) 610 1400. www.virukeskus.com. Open: 9am–9pm.

Reval Antique

This is one of the city's better antique shops, selling icons, silver, clocks and watches, porcelain, medals, toys and dolls.
Harju 13. Tel: (372) 644 0747. Open: Mon–Fri 10am–6pm, Sat 10am–5pm.

Reet Aus

This fashion store offers cutting-edge design from some of Estonia's newest talents.
Muurihave 19 (no tel). Open: Mon–Sat 10am–6pm, Sun 11am–5pm.

The St Martin's Day Fair, organised in Tallinn in mid-November each year by the Estonian Folk Art and Craft Union, offers national handicraft workshops and sales, with craftspeople in traditional costumes, folk music, dancing and typical Estonian food.
Estonian Folk Art and Craft Union. Tel: (372) 660 4772. www.folkart.ee

Baltic amber

Jewellery made from glistening, honey-hued amber is one of the best buys in Estonia. Amber is the fossilised resin of ancient conifers that has undergone profound chemical changes after lying underground for millions of years, and the world's largest deposits are found around the coasts of the Baltic Sea, where it may have lain buried in sand for up to 60 million years.

Amber comes in a wide range of shapes and colours, from pebble-shaped lumps to rods or tear-drops, and in colours that range from translucent yellow to deep reddish-orange to milky white, the most translucent. Insects and plants which were trapped in the sticky resin before it became fossilised are often found perfectly preserved in beads of amber, and have provided scientists with a wealth of information.

Some have suggested that ancient genetic material preserved in such specimens could enable us to re-create life forms that have been extinct for many millions of years – an idea that inspired the film *Jurassic Park*, in which dinosaurs and other long-vanished monsters from the deep past were cloned from DNA

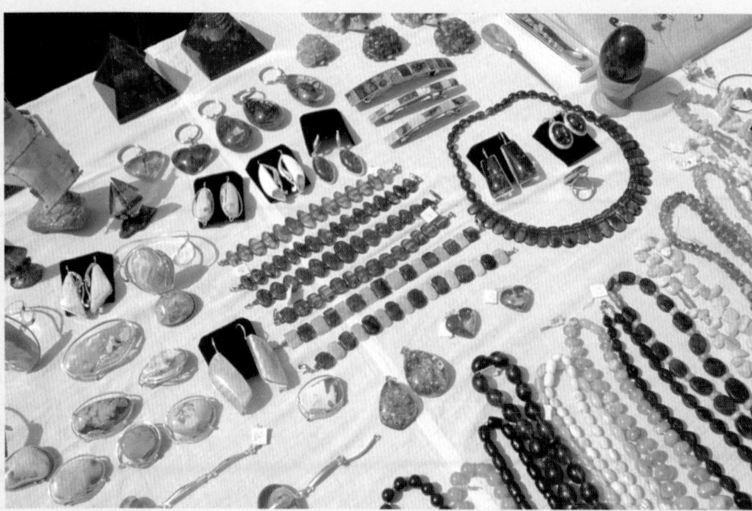

Baltic amber on sale

Amber displayed in a jewellery store

samples extracted from amber fossils. Sadly, that idea has been thoroughly de-bunked by serious scientists.

Fragments of amber are sometimes washed up on Estonian beaches after winter storms, and amber amulets and ornaments carved by Stone Age people, Viking traders and early Estonian settlers are sometimes found at archaeological sites.

Cheaper amber jewellery in Estonia is made from 'amberoid' or pressed amber, by fusing smaller fragments of inferior amber into larger pieces; amberoid can be easily identified by the parallel bands that betray its semi-artificial origins.

When rubbed with a piece of cloth or silk, amber develops a static electrical charge and attracts very light objects such as feathers or scraps of silk. The ancient Greeks discovered this unusual property more than 2,000 years ago, and the word 'electricity' is derived from their name for amber, *elektron*.

The amber which was prized by the Greeks and other Mediterranean peoples came from the Baltic region, and amber was one of the treasures of the northern world that were carried south and east by Swedish Viking traders along the river trade routes across Russia to Constantinople, capital of the Byzantine Empire.

One of the treasures of imperial St Petersburg was a reception room decorated throughout in Baltic amber. It was presented to Peter the Great by Frederick, King of Prussia, in 1716 and was said to be a masterpiece of baroque art, with amber walls and ceiling panels in which were reflected the glow of more than 500 candles. Catherine the Great had the room moved from Peter's Winter Palace to her summer residence at Tsarskoye Selo, just outside St Petersburg. After the German invasion of Russia in 1941, the Amber Room was dismantled and shipped to Königsberg (now Kaliningrad). During the fall of the city to the Red Army in 1941, its treasures vanished, and have never been recovered. The most likely explanation is that they were destroyed by fire during an air raid, but there are persistent rumours that they are still concealed somewhere in Germany or Russia.

Children

Estonia in summer has plenty to occupy and entertain families with older, active children, though the country as a whole is not an ideal destination for toddlers and younger kids. Tallinn's medieval towers and city walls will delight children who enjoyed the sword-and-sorcery adventures of Harry Potter *or* The Lord of the Rings. *Tallinn has some purpose-built attractions for children, but in general Estonia makes no special allowances for younger visitors.*

Facilities such as highchairs in restaurants or secure child seats in rental cars are widely available. Above all, however, Estonia's long hours of summer daylight favour an outdoor summer culture that is great for family holidays. It offers plenty of family accommodation in country cottages, guesthouses and apartments, and a very wide range of activities on land, lakes, rivers and at sea, including cycling, canoeing and kayaking, fishing, sailing and boating. Estonia's flat terrain makes it ideal for family cycling trips, and cross-country skiing and sledging are popular in winter.

Art galleries

Kullo Children's Gallery

This gallery, housed in a medieval house in Tallinn's Old Town, holds workshops for budding artists and hangs works by young Estonian painters, many of them in their teens or even younger.

Roheline aas 3. Tel: (372) 644 6873. www.kullo.ee. Open: Wed–Mon 10am–5pm. Closed: Tue. Admission charge.

Beaches

There are plenty of places to play in and on the waters of the Baltic, with beaches and water-sports centres not far from Tallinn and on the Gulf of Finland and Gulf of Rīga coasts. The Baltic is a shallow and almost tideless sea, and its calm, surprisingly warm water is ideal for children in summer. Rowing boats can be rented at Pirita, only a few minutes from central Tallinn. West of Tallinn (24–40km/15–25 miles from the city) there are beaches at Vääna-Jõesuu, Lohusalu and Lahepera Bay. Western Estonia also has beaches on the sheltered Gulf of Rīga, including Jarverand on the Saaremaa coast at Kuressaare.

Cinemas

Estonia's largest cinema is the Coca Cola Plaza, with 11 screens, at least one of

which is usually showing recently released English-language movies suitable for children (with Estonian subtitles).
Hobujaama 4, Tallinn.
www.superkinod.ee

Museums

By far the best place to take children in Tallinn is the Estonian Open-Air Museum (*see p47*), a huge park filled with more than 70 old-fashioned wooden buildings, thatched cottages, farm buildings, a village school, horse-drawn carriage rides and a traditional village tavern serving Estonian meals.

Nearby, on the outskirts of Tallinn at Pirita, the Estonian History Museum's annexe at Marjamae Palace is housed in a grandiose mock-Gothic mansion, and takes a look at life in 19th-century Estonia (*Pirita tee 56; tel: (372) 601 4535; www.eam.ee; open: Wed–Sun 11am–6pm; admission charge*).

Tallinn also has a quota of offbeat museums – mostly relics of the solemn educational policies of the Soviet era – that may amuse and entertain curious kids.

Doll Museum

This quirky little collection features a permanent exhibition of dolls, puppets, marionettes, wooden and lead soldiers and other toys, including hand-made wooden figures and rag dolls and beautifully costumed 19th-century china dolls.
Kotzebue 16. Tel: (372) 641 3491.
www.linnamuuseum.ee. Open: Wed–Sun 11am–5pm. Admission charge.

Cycling enthusiasts enjoying a ride in the sun

Energia Centre

Housed in a former power-generating station, the Science and Technology Centre was originally designed to celebrate the achievements of Soviet scientists and engineers, and its space exploration section still pays greater tribute to Soviet cosmonauts than NASA astronauts. Slightly old-fashioned compared with similar attractions in the West, but still good fun, with lots of see-and-do displays to entertain enquiring young minds.

Põhja pst. 29. Tel: (372) 715 2650. www.energiakeskus.ee. Open: Mon–Sat 10am–5pm. Closed: Sun. Admission charge.

Fire-Fighting Museum

With a rather heavy hand, this museum hammers home lessons against playing with fire, with grim displays of fire-scorched homes and photos of fire victims. Less gruesomely, it features fire-fighting equipment through the ages, from the primitive leather buckets used by medieval volunteers to the protective gear of Soviet fire crews. There is even a miniature house that illustrates dozens of ways to accidentally set your home on fire

Vana-Viru 14. Tel: (372) 644 4251. www.rescue.ee. Open: Tue–Sat noon–5pm. Closed: Sun & Mon. Admission charge.

Toomas the Train

This dinky tourist train makes a 20-minute tour through Tallinn's cobbled Old Town streets and is ideal for families sightseeing with toddlers and smaller children.

Departs from Kuninga tanav near Raekoja plats (opposite Olde Hansa Restaurant) hourly, May–Sept Mon–Sat noon–6pm, Sun 11am–6pm. May be cancelled on very wet days. Admission charge.

TV Tower (Teletorn)

This 314m (1,030ft) triumph of Soviet engineering (it opened in 1980) is one of the few Soviet relics that is regarded with some grudging affection. Children will be awestruck by the view from the observation deck of the restaurant-bar – in clear weather you can see most of Estonia and all the way across to Finland.

Kloostrimetsa 58a. Tel: (372) 623 8250. www.teletorn.ee. Open: daily 10am–midnight. Admission charge.

Parks

Tallinn has plenty of green space where children can play and adults can relax, including the botanical gardens with hundreds of plants from all over the world, the city zoo, and a leafy estate once laid out for a Russian czar.

Tallinn Botanical Garden

Families can explore Estonia's natural heritage without leaving Tallinn with a visit to the Botanical Garden, where some 8,000 plant species are nurtured, along with greenhouses that shelter tropical, subtropical and desert plants.

A good place to take kids on a rainy day.
Bus 34 or 38 to Kloostrimetsa.
Kloostrimetsa tee 52. Tel: (372) 606 2666. Open: daily 11am–4pm. Admission charge.

Kadriorg Park

The wooded park is northwest of Weizenbergi in the garden suburb of Kadriorg, east of central Tallinn. The huge park is traversed by a network of paths and trails where children can play. The Swan Pond on Weizenbergi is a favourite rendezvous for Tallinn families, with a flock of friendly ducks quite used to being fed by toddlers.
Tram 1 or 3 to Kadriorg.
Weizenbergi. No tel or web. Open: daily, daylight hours. Admission free.

Tallinn Zoo

The Zoo houses animals from Estonia and the Arctic regions, including Siberian tigers and bears, as well as some exotic species such as elephants, crocodiles, apes and monkeys.
Bus 22 or Tram 6, 7 or 8 to Zoo.
Paldiski mantee 145. Tel: (372) 694 3300. www.tallinnzoo.ee. Open: May–Sept 9am–7pm, Oct–Apr 9am–3pm. Admission charge.

National parks

Lahemaa National Park is the most accessible of Estonia's nature reserves, and an ideal family destination with picturesque bays, lakes and streams, and a range of activities including kayaking, sailing and cycling and a variety of walking trails (*see pp58–62*).

National Puppet Theatre

Children of all ages (and their parents) will find the marionette performances of the Estonian National Puppet Theatre entrancing. There are programmes in English as well as regular performances in Estonian (*see website for timings*).
Lai 1, Tallinn. Tel: (372) 667 9555 (box office). www.nukuteater.ee. Open: daily 10am–6pm.

A quiet beach in Lahemaa National Park

Entertainment

Throughout Estonia, music is one of the most popular forms of entertainment, with drinking a close second. During the Soviet era, Tallinn was a popular destination for groups of Finns who arrived by ferry for weekend bouts of cheap beer and vodka. In post-Soviet Estonia, Tallinn has established itself as one of Europe's most popular destinations for groups of young people in search of a good time, and boasts dozens of bars, clubs and music venues catering to all tastes.

The capital also has a number of casinos and cinemas showing foreign films with Estonian subtitles. Outside the capital, entertainment is much more low-key, with just a handful of music bars and discos in towns such as Tartu and Pärnu. Summer, however, sees a busy festival calendar, with numerous rock, jazz and folk festivals, especially in July and August. The indispensable guide to entertainment in Tallinn and elsewhere is *Tallinn This Week*, published weekly in English and offering a comprehensive guide to what to see and where to go. It is available free from hotels and tourist information offices. *Tallinn In Your Pocket* (EEK35), published six times a year, is also an excellent guide.

Tallinn's bar and club scene is very active, with music bars serving up drinks and live entertainment from cocktails and salsa to rum and reggae or Guinness and Irish folk music. Friday is Tallinn's liveliest night out, when the partying goes on from around 10pm until about 6am.

TALLINN'S SLEAZY SIDE

Independence ended decades of Soviet censorship of every aspect of life in Estonia. One of the less attractive results has been a boom in sleazy nightlife – Tallinn boasts dozens of striptease and 'private dancer' clubs, some of which are marginally more tasteful than others. Popular with bachelor groups and straying business travellers, these establishments serve very expensive drinks and are adept at adding an array of unexpected extras to your bill.

TALLINN

Bars and clubs

Angel

The biggest venue for Tallinn's gay scene is lively, steamy and raunchy, with live divas and DJs and fashionable drinks.

Sauna 1. Tel (372) 641 6880. www.clubangel.ee. Café open: Mon–Wed noon–2am, Thur–Fri noon–4am, Sun 2pm–1am. Club open: Wed–Sat 10pm–5am (strict door policy).

Bar Bogart

On the second floor of the posh Hotel Viru, this is a comfortable and stylish place for an early- or late-evening drink. *Sokos Hotel Viru, Viru väljak 4. Tel: (372) 680 9380. Open: 9pm–3am.*

Beer House

This cavernous beer hall (complete with German brass band music) and disco in Tallinn Old Town even has its own private saunas. *Dunkri 5. Tel: (372) 627 6520. www.beerhouse.ee. Open: Mon–Thur 10pm–midnight, Fri & Sat 10pm–2am.*

BonBon

BonBon is a very busy and extremely popular club with a reputation as Tallinn's hottest dance venue, but anyone over 40 may feel a little out of place here. *Mere 5. Tel: (372) 661 6080. www.bonbon.ee. Open: Wed, Fri & Sat 11pm–4am.*

Bonnie and Clyde

More stylish, more relaxed and less crowded than Tallinn's throbbing downtown discos, the Olümpia Hotel nightclub attracts a more mature crowd. *Reval Olümpia Hotel, Liivalaia 33. Tel: (372) 631 5333. www.revalhotels.com. Open: 9pm–3am.*

Café Amigo

Tallinn's most stylish and relaxed nightspot offers free admission to guests at its parent hotel and attracts locals too. Frequent live performances by Estonian bands. *Sokos Hotel Viru, Viru väljak 4. Tel: (372) 631 5333. www.amigo.ee. Open: 9pm–4am.*

Café VS

This large and popular bar has plenty of seating, chilled-out sounds after midnight and also serves surprisingly good Indian food. The combination makes it popular

People gather in the Old Town Square in Tallinn for a night out

Nimeta Baar in Tallinn is a favourite with expatriates

with Tallinn expatriates, tourists and locals.
Pärnu mantee 2. Tel: (372) 627 2627. www.cafevs.ee. Open: Mon–Thur 10am–1am, Fri 10am–3am, Sat noon–3am & Sun noon–1am.

Guitar Safari
Don your old black leather jacket for a nostalgic visit to Tallinn's longest-established rock and blues club, in an appropriately dark Old Town basement venue which hosts Estonian and international (mainly European) pub-rock bands.
Muurihave 22. Tel: (372) 641 1607. Open: Mon–Fri noon–3am, Sat 2pm–3am, Sun 1pm–3am.

Hookah House
Extremely fashionable, this restaurant-lounge may suffer from the ban on smoking in restaurants, and certainly anyone who wants a puff on one of its signature hubble-bubble pipes of flavoured tobacco now has to take it outside. Dance music from DJs every evening.
Roosikrantsi 3. Tel: (372) 644 2266. Open: Mon–Thur 10am–11pm, Fri–Sat 10am–2am.

Lounge 24
Apart from the café-restaurant halfway up the TV Tower, this sophisticated bar on the 24th level of the posh Radisson SAS hotel has the best view in town, with an open-air terrace for sunny evenings.
Radisson SAS Hotel, Ravala 3. Tel: (372) 682 3424. Open: noon–2am.

Molly Malone's
Molly Malone's is the doyenne of Tallinn's Irish-themed pubs, with a central location just off Town Hall

Square, a handy rendezvous for visitors. It generally attracts an older crowd, with rock, pop and folk bands at weekends.
Mundi 2. Tel: (372) 631 3016. www.baarid.ee. Open: 11am–2am.

Nimeta Baar
This is 'The Pub With No Name' (how original) and is a favourite with younger locals and visitors, with a tiny dance floor, potent cocktails (usually two for the price of one) and samba music.
Suur-Karja 13. Tel: (372) 620 9299. Open: Mon–Thur 11am–2am, Fri–Sat 11am–4am, Sun noon–2am.

Cinemas
Cinemas are popular in Estonia, where not everyone can afford satellite television and the choice of terrestrial TV channels is limited. Tallinn and other large towns have cinemas showing recent releases in English with Estonian subtitles.

Coca Cola Plaza
Estonia's largest cinema, with 11 screens, shows a mix of international blockbusters and Estonian movies.
Hobujaama 4, Tallinn. www.superkinod.ee.

Cinema Soprus
This recently opened art-house cinema shows new and old Estonian films and alternative work by some of the more imaginative contemporary European film-makers.
Vana-Posti 8, Tallinn. Tel: (372) 644 1919. www.kino.ee

Classical music and opera
Estonia has a rich tradition of classical music, and there are frequent performances in Tallinn by the Estonian National Symphony Orchestra and visiting ensembles. See *Tallinn This Week* for performances.

Estonia Concert Hall
The Estonia Concert Hall is Estonia's largest and most prestigious venue for performances of classical music and is the home of the Estonian National Symphony Orchestra.
Estonia pst 4, Tallinn. Tel: (372) 614 7700. www.concert.ee. Bookings from noon–7pm weekdays or noon–5pm Sat. Most performances begin at 7pm.

Estonian National Opera
Next to the Concert Hall is the Estonia Theatre, home of the Estonian National Opera, which celebrated its 100th season in 2005. It performs operas in their original language. The interior of this attractive Art Nouveau building – which was rebuilt after bomb damage in 1944 – has recently been completely restored, resulting in greatly improved acoustics.
Estonia pst 4, Tallinn. Tel: (372) 683 1215. www.opera.ee. Box office open: Mon–Sun noon–7pm. Most performances start at 7pm.

Tallinn Town Hall
Tallinn's imposing Town Hall is frequently used as a venue for classical concerts and musical evenings. It also allows the visitor a chance to relish the building's splendid interior.
Raekoja plats 1. Tel: (372) 645 7900. Performances begin at 6pm.

Other classical music venues include:
Niguliste Museum and Concert Hall
Niguliste 13. Tel: (372) 644 9911. www.ekm.ee. Most performances begin at 7pm.
Kadriorg Palace
Weizenbergi 37. Tel: (372) 606 6400. www.ekm.ee. Most performances begin at 6pm.

Jazz

Basso
Live jazz plays on Thursday nights at this chic wine and cocktail lodge, and recorded jazz is played most other nights. This is one of Tallinn's more elegant café-bars.
Pikk 13. Tel: (372) 641 9312. Open: Mon–Fri 11am–1am, Fri–Sat 11am–2am, Sun 11am–midnight.

Martini Jazz Café
Phone or check the website of this little bar to find out who's playing and when. Get there early or book a table, as it's often crowded on live jazz nights.
Vaike-Karja 1. Tel: (372) 533 0002. www.martinijazzcafe.ee. Open: Mon–Thur 11am–11pm, Fri–Sat 11am–3am, Sun 11am–6pm.

PÄRNU

Pärnu, on the coast, comes into its own in the summer months when it becomes a popular nightlife destination for young Estonians. Nightlife virtually dies during the winter months, when many establishments close or move to winter venues in Tartu or Tallinn. Higher culture is provided during the Pärnu Days of Contemporary Music in mid-January and the David Oistrakh Festival of contemporary and classical music in early July. For information on both these, see the website *www.ooper.pärnu.ee*

Bars and clubs

Night Club Tallinn
The loudest and liveliest club outside Tallinn moves to Pärnu's Kursaal venue for the summer.
Mere pst 22. Tel: (372) 446 4616. www.clubtallinn.ee. Open: June–Aug Wed–Sat 11pm–3am.

Classical music

Pärnu Concert Hall
Pärnu's grand concert hall has excellent acoustics and is the venue for regular (fortnightly) performances by the Estonian National Symphony Orchestra and by other orchestras and ensembles.
Aida 4. Tel: (372) 445 5800. www.concert.ee

TARTU

Tartu, with its youthful student population, also has a good sprinkling of bars offering live music, and is second only to the capital as a venue for classical and traditional music and dance.

Bars and clubs

Night Club Tallinn

For full-on nightlife and loud music, Night Club Tallinn is Tartu's top spot (and claims to be the best nightclub not just in Estonia but in all the Baltic States). Popular with students, the club moves to its summer venue in Pärnu (*see p154*) when the university term ends.

Narva mantee 27. Tel: (372) 740 3157. www.clubtallinn.ee. Open: Sept–June Wed–Sat 11pm–3am.

Who Doesn't Like Johnny Depp?

Tartu's newest nightlife venue opened in 2007 and hosts live bands and DJs.

Kompanii 2. Tel: (372) 502 6076. Open: Wed–Sat 10pm–4am.

Wilde

A comfortable, spacious pub favoured by Tartu students, university staff and other intellectuals, with draught beers and a good choice of vodka.

Vallikraavi 4. Tel: (372) 730 9764. Open: Mon–Tue noon–midnight, Wed–Thur noon–1am, Fri–Sat noon–2am, Sun 1pm–midnight.

Classical music

Vanemuine Concert Hall

Tartu's most important venue for performances by leading Estonian and international music, opera, drama and ballet ensembles.

Vanemuise 6. Tel: (372) 744 0165. www.vanemuine.ee. Box office open: Mon–Sat 10am–7pm. Most performances start at 7pm.

The National Opera House

Sport and leisure

Estonia has a wide assortment of activities for lovers of sports and the outdoors, especially in summer. The best time of year to enjoy the country's range of leisure activities is from May to September, when the weather is warm and often sunny and there are long hours of daylight, but the Estonian countryside also offers a range of winter-sports activities.

Canoeing (*see p134*)

Estonian Canoeing Federation
Aasa 1, Tartu. Tel: (372) 740 0599. e-mail: koitp@hot.ee

Cycling

The Estonian Cycling Route Network is a joint project between the Vanta Aga Cycling Club, Estonian Tourist Board, the Ministry of the Environment, the Road Administration and regional authorities, and will be part of the EuroVelo network of long-distance routes across Europe.

Klubi Tartu Maraton, based in Tartu, holds the Tartu Rattaralli cycle road races over 137km (85-mile) and 71km (44-mile) courses as well as a mountain bike marathon over the Otepää-Elva ski trail in summer (*see p159*).
Laulupeo puiestee 25, Tartu. Tel: (372) 742 1644. www.tartumaraton.ee

Estonian Cycling Federation
Pirita tee 12, Tallinn. Tel: (372) 603 1545. www.ejl.ee

Fishing

With its long Baltic coastline and a vast number of lakes, ponds, streams and rivers, Estonia offers tremendous opportunities for recreational angling in a wide range of conditions, and for more than a dozen fish species. You may fish anywhere without a permit, using a simple hand line which consists of a rod and line not more than 1½ times the length of the rod, a single hook, float and sinkers. A temporary permit is required if using a spinning reel. The price of a fishing permit is the same throughout Estonia and permits can be bought at any county Environmental Department.

Golf

Golf is an increasingly popular sport in Estonia. New 18-hole courses have opened on Saaremaa (*www.saaremaagolf.ee*) and at Otepää (*www.otepaagolf.ee*). The new Estonian Golf and Country Club at Manniva, 24km (15 miles) from central Tallinn, has a dramatic location with mature oak trees, prehistoric relics, old stone walls and numerous ponds. Among its hazards is the 40m (130ft) height difference to contend with.

Estonian Golf and Country Club
Jõelähtme, Manniva village.
Tel: (372) 666 2121. www.egcc.ee

Estonian Golf Association
Narva 24, Tallinn. www.golf.ee

Hiking

The Estonian State Forest Management Centre (RMK) manages a network of forest hiking trails and recreation areas with campsites, forest lodges, picnic and campfire spots in ten of Estonia's most beautiful regions.

State Forest Management Centre
Tel: (372) 628 1500. www.rmk.ee

Horse riding

Horse riding is a lovely way to see the Estonian countryside in winter or summer, and several riding centres and tourist farms offer horse and pony trips, carriage rides in summer and horse-drawn sleigh rides in winter.

Northern Estonia:

Kivisaare Ratsatalu
Järve 10, Aegviidu, Harju.
Tel: (372) 566 31520.
www.jb.ee/ratsatalu

Rebala Tallid
Rebala, Jõelähtme, Harju
Tel: (372) 529 7760.
www.rebalatallid.com

Saue Riding Club
Pärnasalu 38, Saue, Harju.
Tel: (372) 679 0888.
www.moisatall.ee

Veskimetsa Riding Centre
Paldiski 135, Tallinn.
Tel: (372) 656 3904.
www.veskimetsa.ee

Southern Estonia:

Sammuli Stables
Vardja Viiratsi vald, Viljandi.
Tel: (372) 526 9100.
www.sammulitallid.ee

Timmo Stables
Mammaste Põlva vald, Põlva.
Tel: (372) 799 8530.
www.kagureis.ee

Enjoy Tallinn by cycling around the city

Western Estonia:
Seeba Holiday Houses
Kassari Käina vald, Hiiumaa.
Tel: (372) 469 7246.
www.hot.ee/seebatalu

Kiiking

Estonia's own unique and dizzying swing-sport has grown out of ancient roots. Kiiking is a new and uniquely Estonian sport which is performed on adult-sized swings. The aim is to propel the swing over the top of its frame, through 360 degrees. Considerable strength and nerve are called for. Records are set based on the length of the shafts of the swing, with the current Guinness World Record being held by the Estonian Andrus Asamae at 7.2m (24ft).

Kiiking is a modern descendant of a very old Estonian pastime, for swinging has very strong traditions in the national culture. There are big wooden swing-platforms, large enough for several adults, in almost every rural village and these are used at almost every summer song festival. Kiiking as a sport began in Pärnu in 1997 and since then has attracted an increasing interest among Estonians and a handful of foreigners. The modern kiik is a high-tech piece of equipment, with a safety harness and wrist and ankle ties to ensure that swingers stay on board even at the top of their trajectory. Swings can be lengthened to increase the challenge.

Estonian Kiiking Federation
Mäepealse tee 9, Metsakasti, Viimsi vald.
Tel: (372) 505 5637. www.kiiking.ee

Sailing

Despite the country's northerly location, Estonian waters are sheltered and can offer good sailing conditions from May to September, but yachting is still quite a new sport, as access to the open sea was denied during Soviet rule. The non-governmental organisation Keep the Estonian Sea Tidy maintains a database of yacht harbours around the coast, ranging from relatively well-served marinas such as those at Pirita and Pärnu and which meet European Union standards, to half-abandoned ports that offer practically no services.

Keep The Estonian Sea Tidy
Pirita tee 17, Tallinn. Tel: (372) 623 9127.
www.hem.ee

Estonian Yachting Federation
1-6K, Regati pst 1-6K Tallinn.
Tel: (372) 639 8960. www.puri.ee

Swimming pools

Several Tallinn hotels, including the Hotel Olümpia and the Pirita Hotel, have pools that are open to guests and club members. The Viimsi Tervis Spa Hotel, just outside Tallinn, has a 25m (82ft) lane pool, a separate pool for children and a whirlpool, and is open to day visitors.

Ranveere tee 11, Viimsi.
Tel: (372) 606 1000. www.vimsispa.ee.
Open: 7am–11pm. Admission charge.

In Tartu, the Aura Centre has a 50m (164ft) pool and a 25m (82ft) beginner's pool.

Turu 10. Tel: (372) 730 0280.
www.aurakeskus.ee.
Open: 7am–11pm.

Tennis

The Rocca al Mare Tennis Club in western Tallinn has 16 tennis courts and four badminton courts as well as aerobics and fitness facilities.

Haabersti 5, Tallinn. Tel: (372) 660 0520.
Open: daily 7am–11pm.

Estonian Tennis Federation

Regati 1, Tallinn. Tel: (372) 639 8635.
www.tennis.ee

Water sports

Several leisure centres offer such water sports as sailing, wake-boarding and water-skiing on Baltic and inland waters. Pärnu is the country's main water-sports destination.

Sun & Fun

This activity-holiday centre offers sailing, motorboats, water-skiing and wake-boarding and sea trips to offshore islands.

Kooli 32, Pärnu. Tel: (372) 506 2903.
www.holidayresort.ee

Winter sports

With its low-lying terrain, Estonia is more suitable for cross-country skiing (known in Estonia as *loppet*).

Fishing in tranquil waters

Tartu is the main winter-sports region, with a permanent ski route, the Tartu Marathon trail, between Otepää and Elva. The annual Tartu Marathon is Estonia's biggest and most popular sporting event and is operated by Klubi Tartu Maraton (MTU), which also holds marathons for runners in summer.

Tartu Marathon Club (MTU)

Laulupeo puiestee 25, Tartu.
Tel: (372) 742 1644.
www.tartumaraton.ee

Food and drink

Estonian food does not rank among the world's great cuisines, and eating out is not a national pastime, although food and drink certainly play a big part in the country's many traditional festivals. Estonia is a small country with a climate and terrain that restrict the range of farm produce, and this is reflected in the fare.

Since independence, the range of places to eat and drink, especially in Tallinn, has become much more varied, with a huge variety of ethnic restaurants complementing local offerings. Unsurprisingly, the national cuisine of neighbouring eastern European countries and other former satellites of the USSR is also strongly represented.

A restaurant in Kuressaare

Almost all table and bar staff speak English (and often German as well), although this is less true in smaller towns and villages. Prices for a meal, with or without alcohol, range from below western European averages in small, simple restaurants to very expensive in smart hotel restaurants and other ostentatious eating places favoured by Estonia's new rich.

Value Added Tax (currently 18 per cent) is added automatically to all bills but service is never included. Many restaurant staff make a large proportion of their earnings from gratuities, so a tip of ten per cent is always appreciated in restaurants. Tipping is not necessary in bars or self-service restaurants and cafés. Outside Tallinn, Tartu and Pärnu, the choice of places to eat is less varied and the menu is also much more limited, relying heavily on pork, sausage, potatoes and cabbage.

For up-to-date restaurant recommendations and reviews, pick up a copy of the invaluable local guide,

Tallinn In Your Pocket, sold in tourist information offices and hotels and published six times a year, or visit its website *www.inyourpocket.com* for up-to-date reviews.

Types of restaurant

American/International

Tallinn's American-style restaurants offer steaks, burgers, Tex-Mex food and beer in familiar surroundings and at moderate prices.

Asian

Tallinn offers a choice of Chinese (and Chinese-inspired), Indian, Japanese and Korean restaurants. Chinese restaurants can also be found in smaller towns.

Buffet restaurants

Self-service lunch cafés and buffet restaurants in Tallinn and elsewhere are favourites with people on the move and are ideal for sightseers who want to save time.

Caucasian

Migrants from the southern republics brought Armenian, Azerbaijani and Georgian cooking to Estonia during the Soviet era and it still thrives, emphasising grilled meat dishes, kebabs and desserts.

Estonian

Estonian restaurants range from cheap and cheerful to expensive and pretentious. The best have more imaginative menus that make the most of wild game and hearty traditional dishes.

European

French, Spanish, Greek, German and Italian restaurants can be found in Tallinn and the visitor will also find Italian-style pizza restaurants in most Estonian towns.

International

All large hotels have restaurants (open to non-residents as well as guests) with menus boasting multi-national influences. Prices range from reasonable to exorbitant.

Indian restaurant in Tallinn

Themed restaurants

Tallinn has a number of eating places with themes ranging from medieval times to rock-and-roll legends.

WHAT TO EAT

Estonian cuisine

Estonian home cooking blends Scandinavian, Germanic and Russian influences. Most hearty peasant dishes reflect a national culture of hard physical work in a cold climate, with plenty of calories and an emphasis on pork, ham, poultry, sausage, potatoes and other root vegetables, thick cream and black rye bread.

Despite Estonia's long coastline, seafood is not a major part of the traditional diet, although salted or pickled herring is a popular appetiser or snack. Freshwater fish from the many lakes and rivers is much more popular, and is usually pan-fried.

Main courses are always accompanied by boiled potatoes, usually with sour cream, and often with pickled carrots, gherkins, cucumber, cauliflower or mushrooms.

Estonians have a sweet tooth and sweet, sticky puddings are often served on their own in cafés as a morning or afternoon snack.

Other favourite snacks include pancakes with a range of sweet and savoury fillings, savoury dumplings and a variety of cakes and buns.

In the better Estonian restaurants, the visitor can expect to find at least some of the following specialities on the menu:

A woman buys smoked fish from a stall at Lake Peipsi

WHAT'S ON THE MENU?

eelroad	appetisers
hapukoor	sour cream
juust	cheese
kala	fish
kalkun	turkey
kana	chicken
kartulid	potatoes
kaste	sauce
koogiviljad	vegetables
leib	bread
liha	meat
lõhe	salmon
porgand	carrot
salatid	salad
sealiha	pork
skink	ham
supid	soup
suupisted	snacks
taimetoidud	vegetarian
veiseliha	beef

Starters

Keel hernestega: cold boiled tongue served with horseradish

Marineeritud angerjas: marinated eel

Raim: salted herring

Sült: sliced pork in aspic

Voorst: sliced sausage

Fish dishes

Ahven: perch

Forell: trout

Haug: pike

Main courses

Karbonaad: battered pork chop

Mulgikapsad: pork and sauerkraut stew

Silgusoust: sprats with bacon in sour cream

Verivorst: black pudding made with pig's blood and barley sausage, traditionally served at Christmas time with redcurrant jelly

Desserts

Kama: sweetened porridge made with mealed rye, oats, barley and peas

Karask: barley bread with raisins and other dried fruit

Mannapuder: semolina pudding

Snacks

Köök: cake

Kringel: sweet fruit loaf

Pankoogid: pancake

Pelmenid: meat or vegetable ravioli

Piruka: cabbage and pork dumpling

Sai: sweet bun

Food for vegetarians

Strict vegetarians will have problems finding acceptable dishes on most Estonian menus, and even those whose diet stretches to include eggs and fish may find choices very limited. Salads often include cold cuts of meat or sausage, and soups are almost always made with meat-based stock. Even cosmopolitan Tallinn has no purely vegetarian restaurants, and ethnic Asian restaurants are the best option for those who do not eat meat.

WHAT TO DRINK

Alcoholic

Estonians are copious beer drinkers and the country produces a number of drinkable brews, including the ubiquitous Saku Originaal. Imported European and American beers are also available on tap or in bottles. Vodka (*viin*) is very popular and is generally drunk chilled and undiluted, often with a beer chaser. Viru Valge and Saaremaa are the best-known vodka labels. Others include Türi, Crystal, Laua and Y2K. Estonia also produces a cloyingly sweet liqueur, Vana Tallinn. Red, white and sparkling wines are imported from main European wine-making countries, and spirits including whisky and brandy are also imported.

Non-alcoholic

Kali is the national non-alcoholic beverage of choice. This slightly fizzy, yeasty drink is a kind of unfermented beer. Nicknamed 'Estonian Coca-Cola', it is an acquired taste. Mineral water is cheap and widely available and is preferable to tap water, which while safe to drink is heavily chlorinated. Ubiquitous carbonated drinks such as the various cola brands are sold everywhere, and Estonians have also acquired a taste for caffeinated soft drinks such as Red Bull and (from Scotland) Irn Bru, which is often mixed with vodka by younger, trendier drinkers.

Tea and coffee

Both tea and coffee (*kohv*) are drunk at any time of day and both are usually served without milk. Filter (or instant) coffee is more common than espresso or cappuccino. For coffee with cream, ask for *kohv koorega.*

BEER IN ESTONIA

Estonia's oldest and biggest brewery, Saku, was founded in 1820. Its leading brand, Saku Originaal, is Estonia's most popular brew and is exported worldwide. The brewery produces more than a dozen beers, ranging from light lagers to darker ales. Rivalling Saku is the Tartu Brewery, which produces the A le Coq lager, Estonia's second-favourite beer. It is slightly sweeter and richer-tasting than Saku Originaal. Tartu Brewery also makes a dark ale, Black Beer. Viru Beer, another long-established brewery from northeast Estonia, makes another dark porter-style beer, Palmse, and a light lager, Toolse. From Saaremaa island comes the potent Saaremaa Ale (alcohol content – 9 per cent!).

WHERE TO EAT

Most Estonian hotels have at least one restaurant, and in Tallinn some of the most prestigious eating places are to be found in the city's luxury hotels. However, Tallinn also offers a huge choice of alternatives which are often very much cheaper than hotel restaurants.

Outside the capital, hotel restaurants are less likely to offer a memorable meal; on the other hand, the range of other options is also likely to be narrower.

In the restaurant listings given below, the star ratings indicate the average cost per person for a meal not including alcohol.

★	less than 65 EEK
★★	65–85 EEK
★★★	85–150 EEK
★★★★	150–200 EEK
★★★★★	More than 200 EEK

Tallinn

Admiral ★★★

Grilled meat and seafood are the main offerings aboard this stylish old steamer moored in Tallinn Harbour. The atmosphere is unforgettable and the food is excellent.

Lootsi 15.

Tel: (372) 662 3777.

Open: noon–11pm.

African Kitchen ★★

The African Kitchen is very different from any other eating place in Tallinn, with a menu full of traditional dishes from all over Africa, a tropical-themed interior, and music at weekends. Popular with young Tallinn-dwellers.

Uus 34.

Tel: (372) 644 2555.

Open: Mon–Thur noon–1am, Fri–Sat noon–2am.

Balthasar ★★

Popular, stylish and central, this restaurant on Town Hall Square specialises in garlic dishes and displays flair and imagination in its menu. The strength of the garlic flavouring in each dish is indicated by the number of bulb symbols next to it on the menu. Reservations recommended.

Raekoja plats 11.

Tel: (372) 627 6400.

Open: noon–midnight.

Le Bonaparte ★★★

This elegant (and costly) restaurant in the Old Town serves some of the best classical French cooking in Tallinn, though it also emphasises local ingredients such as elk and wild boar.

Beer House, Tallinn

Pikk 45.
Tel: (372) 646 4444.
Open: noon–midnight.

Eesti Maja ★★★
One of the best places in Tallinn to sample real Estonian home cooking with dishes like eel, black pudding, *mulgikapsad* and more in a friendly, family atmosphere. The buffet lunch is excellent value and a great time-saver for sightseers.
Lauteri 1.
Tel: (372) 645 5252.
Open: 11am–11pm.

Egoist ★★★★★
The most expensive and exclusive restaurant in Tallinn is dedicated to pampering its diners. Lunch or dinner here is as near to an unforgettable culinary experience as you will find in Estonia.
Vene 33.
Tel: (372) 646 4052.
Open: noon–midnight.

Gloria ★★★★★
Tallinn's oldest and most prestigious restaurant, opened in 1937, is a favourite with the rich and famous, with an opulent interior and a menu and wine list to match. Reservations are essential.
Muurihave 2.
Tel: (372) 644 6950.

Kompressor ★
With a big choice of sweet and savoury pancakes, this is an excellent, filling option for those on a small budget.
Rataskaeva 3.
Tel: (372) 646 4210.
Open: daily 11am–midnight.

Kuldse Nortsu Kõrts ★★★★
Its name means 'the Golden Piglet Inn' and this lively country-style restaurant in one of the capital's main hotels (only 100m/110yds from Town Hall Square). It has a big menu of traditional pork dishes and other favourites. It also offers a better than average choice for vegetarians.
Dunkri 8.
Tel: (372) 628 6567.
Open: noon–midnight.

Olde Hansa ★★★
This restaurant in the heart of the Old Town re-creates the world of medieval Reval (Tallinn) with re-invented medieval recipes, costumed waiters and waitresses, chamber music and candlelight. It may be a little kitsch, but it is great fun.
Vana turg 1.
Tel: (372) 627 9020.
Open: 11am–midnight.

Texas Honky Tonk Cantina ★★
Cold American beer, tequila and other shots, burgers, tacos, chilli and other Tex-Mex dishes are on the menu in this western-themed restaurant that is popular with expats and visitors.
Pikk 43.
Tel: (372) 631 1755.
Open: noon–midnight.

Vanaema Juures ★★
Wild boar, elk, venison and other game appear on the menu in season here, along with other roast and grilled meat dishes. Furnished with antiques, the restaurant has a truly Estonian atmosphere.
Rataskaevu 10.
Tel: (372) 626 9080.
Open: noon–10pm.

Northern Estonia

Rondeel ★★
This restaurant in a corner tower of Narva Castle has an outdoor

terrace for summer dining and its menu includes Estonian and international dishes.
Peterburi tee 2, Narva.
Tel: (372) 359 9257.
Open: 10am–10pm.

Sagadi Manor ★★
Housed in a former aristocratic manor house, this restaurant serves traditional dishes and freshly baked bread. It also offers cycle hire, forest trail guides, and hostel and hotel-style accommodation.
Sagadi, Vihula vald, Lääne-Virumaa.
Tel: (372) 676 7888.
Open: noon–10pm.

Saka Cliff Hotel and Spa ★★
A hotel restaurant that specialises in Russian dishes, with a limited choice of Estonian and western dishes on the menu.
Saka mõis, Kohtla vald, Ida-Viru.
Tel: (372) 336 4900.
Open: noon–9pm.

Valga Laev Hotel and Restaurant ★★
Close to the ferry harbour, this small hotel restaurant is the best (indeed virtually the only) option for eating out in the former Soviet garrison town of Paldiski.
Rae 32, Paldiski.
Tel: (372) 674 2035.
Open: noon–10pm.

Southern Estonia

Anna Sophia ★★★
The elegant à la carte restaurant of the

Olde Hansa re-creates medieval Reval

Taagepera Castle Hotel is a surprising discovery in the rural setting of southern Valga county. An excellent array of Estonian and western dishes.
Taagepera küla, Helme vald, Valga. Tel: (372) 766 6390. Open: noon–10pm.

Bernhard Hotel ★★★
This hotel restaurant in the heart of Estonia's winter sports region offers a good choice of

A restaurant in Pärnu

traditional Estonian dishes, international choices, and, unusually for an Estonian eating place, a children's menu. In summer, there is alfresco dining with barbecued dishes made to order.
Kolga tee 22a, Otepää.
Tel: (372) 766 9600.
Open: noon–11pm.

Goldfish ⭑
This fish restaurant specialises in freshly caught trout, perch, pike and eel from Lake Peipsi and other rivers and lakes nearby.
Raja Kasepää vald, Jõgeva valdo.
Tel: (372) 516 5540.
Open: May–Sept 10am–10pm, Oct–Apr 9am–9pm.

Restaurant Volga ⭑⭑
Opened in 2007, this Art Deco restoration of one of the town's grandest old cafés is Tartu's largest and poshest eating place, serving Russian and French dishes.
Kuutri 1.
Tel: (372) 730 5444.
Open: Mon–Thur 11am–11pm, Fri–Sat 11am–midnight.

Western Estonia

Ammende Villa ⭑⭑⭑
This opulent hotel restaurant in Pärnu is within an attractive Art Nouveau building and serves French and Mediterranean dishes accompanied by wines from a surprisingly extensive list from France, Germany, Italy and Spain.
Mere 7, Pärnu.
Tel: (372) 447 3888.
Open: noon–11pm.

Arenburg ⭑⭑
The restaurant of Saaremaa's Hotel Arenburg, near the castle on the main street, serves local dishes, game and international dishes.
Lossi 15, Kuressaare, Saaremaa.
Tel: (372) 452 4728.
Open: daily noon–midnight.

Monus Margarita ⭑⭑
Tex-Mex food and beer, western décor and a friendly staff and cheerful youngish local clientele make this Pärnu restaurant one of the seaside town's better choices.
Akadeemia 5, Pärnu.
Tel: (372) 443 0927.
Open: 11am–1am.

Postipoiss Tavern ⭑⭑⭑
The food at this Russian-themed restaurant in Pärnu is excellent, featuring Slavic favourites and a range of grilled meat and fish dishes. Waiters and waitresses are dressed in traditional costume and there is live music on weekend evenings in summer.
Vee 12, Pärnu.
Tel: (372) 446 4864.
Open: Sun–Thur noon–11.30pm, Fri–Sat noon–2am.

Pädaste Mõis ⭑⭑ **(SeaHouse Restaurant)**
The restaurant of the gracious old Pädaste Manor on Muhu Island favours fresh, locally sourced produce and grows its own herbs in the manor garden. The menu combines Estonian local traditions with a modern approach to food preparation.
Pädaste Muhu vald, Saare.
Tel: (372) 454 8800.
Open: May–Sept noon–3pm & 6–10pm.

Hotels and accommodation

In 1991 Estonia had only a handful of hotels – all in Tallinn, and all operated by the USSR's tourism agency, Intourist. Standards of service, food and comfort were dismal, and prices were set artificially high.

Since then, the accommodation scene has changed very much for the better. International investment, construction and management companies have been welcomed and new ventures have flourished.

Existing hotels and guesthouses have been privatised and modernised (or in some cases demolished and rebuilt) and the variety of places to stay increases each year.

Generally, accommodation outside Tallinn is less sophisticated and luxurious, but there are plenty of reasonably priced smaller hotels in provincial towns.

Standards

Hotels are graded from one to five stars by the Estonian Hotel and Restaurant Association. Even one-star hotels must have en-suite shower and WC.

The fancy Ranna Hotel in Pärnu

Prices are a fair guide to the level of facilities and service you can expect to receive. For 2,500 EEK or above for a double room, the guest can expect the equivalent of five-star international standards. Those who absolutely insist on guaranteed luxury should choose the security of an international brand such as Radisson, the Scandinavian group which runs Tallinn's best hotel.

Types of accommodation

Bed and breakfast

Accommodation with breakfast in private homes, farmhouses or apartments.

Guesthouses

Must have at least five rooms and offer meals (though not necessarily a full-service restaurant).

Holiday homes and visitors' apartments

Cottages, houses and flats with cooking facilities that can be rented individually, usually by the week.

Holiday villages

Basic accommodation services in self-catering bungalows or cabins, with spaces for tents and caravans and parking sites.

Hostels

Simple shared accommodation for hikers, cyclists and budget travellers, offering dining or cooking facilities.

Meriton Old Town Hotel

Hotels

Hotels in Estonia must have at least ten rooms, high standards and at least one restaurant. All have en-suite bathroom and WC and many have a sauna, but few one- to three-star hotels have baths.

Motels

Roadside accommodation with at least ten rooms, hotel-style facilities, plus a secure parking site.

Tourist farms

Usually offer guesthouse, cottage or hostel accommodation, farm cooking and a range of rural activities.

WHERE TO STAY

Estonia has a range of accommodation to suit all budgets. The star ratings indicate the price for a double or twin room per night. Prices do not change seasonally.

★	Budget (Under €100) 600–1,200 EEK
★★	Moderate/ Standard (€100–150) 1,200–2,000 EEK
★★★	Expensive/ Luxury (€150–350) Over 2,200 EEK

Tallinn

Barons ★★★
Built in the 1930s and lovingly restored, Barons has plenty of period atmosphere coupled with attentive service and modern luxury.
Suur-Karja 7.
Tel: (372) 699 9700.
www.baronshotel.ee

Best Western Hotel Tallinn ★★★
This hotel is a standard-setter for the new Tallinn, and has won awards for its stylish redesign of the old Soviet department store building. It has comfortable rooms and meets all international standards.
Laikmaa 5.
Tel: (372) 630 0800.
www.tallinn.ee

Merchant's House Hotel ★★★
Just off Raekoja plats, this elegant 37-bedroom townhouse hotel is housed in a historic building, has a charming garden courtyard, a fine restaurant, sauna, valet parking and other luxuries.
Dunkri 4/6.
Tel: (372) 697 7500.
www.merchantshousehotel.com

Meriton Old Town Hotel ★★
This modern, medium-sized hotel in the Old Town offers very good value for money and is conveniently located.
Lai 49.
Tel: (372) 613 1300.
www.meritonhotels.com

Metropol Hotel ★★
Well-located hotel with modern facilities (including en-suite saunas) and attractive views of the Old Town and the waterfront. The Metropol is housed in a converted 19th-century warehouse building and has plenty of atmosphere.
Mere pst 8b.
Tel: (372) 667 4500.
www.metropol.ee

Reval Hotel Olümpia ★★★
This is an outstanding hotel with great leisure facilities, close to the waterfront and only ten minutes on foot from the Old Town. The service matches up to the facilities.
Liivalaia 33.
Tel: (372) 631 5333.
www.revalhotels.com

Radisson SAS Hotel Tallinn ★★★
Overall, probably the finest hotel in Estonia, this 24-storey hotel is also the country's tallest building. By far the best choice for the business traveller, it also has excellent leisure facilities, including a health club and sauna, and the rooms have breathtaking views of the city.
Rävala pst 3.
Tel: (372) 682 3000.
www.radissonsas.com

Savoy Boutique Hotel ★★★
Renovated in 2006, this is one of the most stylish hotels in Tallinn, with 43 rooms in the heart of the Old Town.
Suur-Karja 17/19.
Tel: (372) 680 6688.
www.savoyhotel.ee

Hotel Schlössle ★★★
One of Tallinn's most character-filled and most expensive hotels, the Schlössle is a grand medieval building that has been fabulously renovated to international luxury standards.
Pühavaimu 13.
Tel: (372) 699 7700.
www.schlossle-hotels.com

Three Sisters ★★★
Rated by some as one of the world's most chic hotels, this establishment is located in three picturesque medieval buildings that have been converted into gorgeous, if costly, places to stay, in the heart of the Old Town.
Pikk 71.
Tel: (372) 630 6300.
www.threesistershotel.com

Uniquestay Mikhli Hotel ★★
Friendly, attractive and businesslike new hotel a short walk from the Old Town and Toompea Hill, with smartly turned-out rooms, sauna, and a fully equipped gym, and free flat-screen PC with broadband internet access in every room.
Endla 23.
Tel: (372) 666 4800.
www.uniquestay.ee

Northern Estonia

Hotel Alex ★★
This is a comfortable, modern hotel with ten double rooms, all with en-suite shower and WC, along with a large restaurant-bar, billiard room and casino. These facilities are popular with locals and the hotel can

The Radisson in New Town, Tallinn

be noisy at weekends.
Kalevia 3, Kohtla-Järve.
Tel: (372) 339 6230.
www.alex.ee

Hotel Inger ★★
This is a comfortable, modern hotel close to the heart of Narva's historic centre, offering 85 rooms and suites, including six deluxe rooms with en-suite sauna.
Pushkini 28, Narva.
Tel: (372) 688 1100.
www.inger.ee

Narva Hotel ★★
Completely renovated before reopening its doors in 2005, the Narva hotel has 50 rooms and offers the most comfortable accommodation in Narva.
Narva Hotel, Pushkini 6, Narva.
Tel: (372) 359 9600.
www.narvahotell.ee

Hotel Wesenbergh ★
This is a pleasant and conveniently located hotel in the centre of one of the region's most attractive towns, with cosy rooms and good facilities.
Tallinna 25, Rakvere.
Tel: (372) 32 23 480.
www.wesenbergh.ee

Hotel Krunk ★★
The hotel Krunk is a small and stylish establishment with 21 rooms (singles and doubles), all with en-suite shower, TV and internet connection. The hotel also has a nine-seat sauna and an adequate restaurant.
Kesk 23, Sillamäe.
Tel: (372) 392 9030.
www.krunk.ee

Southern Estonia

Pühäjarve Spa Hotel ★★★
Swimming pool, gym, saunas, a health centre, a range of sports and lakeside beaches are among the facilities in this well-appointed hotel on the outskirts of Otepää. A good base for skiing in winter or cycling, hiking or boating in summer.
Pühäjarve, Otepää.
Tel: (372) 766 5500.
www.pyhajarve.com

Barclay Hotel ★★
The former Red Army headquarters building has been converted into an agreeable hotel with all the modern conveniences for lesiure and business travellers.
Ülikooli 8, Tartu.
Tel: (372) 744 7100.
www.barclay.ee

Draakon ★★★
The Draakon is Tartu's leading hotel, with a location next to the historic Town Hall, in the very centre of the city. It is housed in a restored classical building and attracts VIP guests.
Raekoja plats 2, Tartu.
Tel: (372) 744 2045.

Hansa Hotell ★★★
This ancient inn, dating back to the heyday of the Hanseatic League of Baltic merchants, has an attractive courtyard and 22 comfortable rooms, as well as a traditional sauna.
Aleksandri 46, Tartu.
Tel: (372) 731 1800.
www.hansahotell.ee

Hotel London ★★
Close to Town Hall Square and the university campus, this is a centrally located, modern hotel with 60 affordably priced rooms, all with TV, minibar and internet connection.
Ruutli 9, Tartu.
Tel (372) 730 5555.
www.londonhotel.ee

Hotel Pallas ★
Just outside the old quarter of Tartu, the Pallas is a pleasant, well-equipped hotel with colourfully decorated rooms and a convenient central location.
Riia 4, Tartu.
Tel: (372) 730 1200.
www.pallas.ee

Taagepera Castle ★★★
Complete with tower and turrets, this historic castle hotel has a great atmosphere as well as excellent facilities, which include a sauna and conference facilities for business visitors.
Taagepere küla, Helme vald, Valgamaa.
Tel: (372) 766 6390.
www.taageperaloss.ee

Western Estonia

Endla Hostel ★
This simple guesthouse in the centre of Haapsalu is close to the railway station and the harbour (for ferries to Hiiumaa) and offers twin- and three-bedded rooms with shared showers, WC and kitchen, and secure parking.
Endla 5, Haapsalu.
Tel: (372) 473 7999.
info@endlahostel.ee

Pihla Tourist Farm ★
Less than 1km (⅔ mile) from Hiiumaa island's landmark, the Kõpu Lighthouse, this cheerful establishment has ten twin-bedded rooms and also offers a range of activities including hiking and fishing, along with its own sauna and internet access.
Pihla talu, Kõpu, Korgessaare, Hiiumaa.
Tel: (372) 469 3491.
www.hot.ee/pihla

Pädaste Manor ★★
This luxurious resort in a historic manor house on the southern tip of Muhu island has spa facilities and a highly rated restaurant. Pädaste is one of Estonia's best country-house hotels.
Pädaste, Muhu vald, Saare. Tel: (372) 454 8800. www.pädaste.ee. Closed: Jan–Feb.

Ammende Villa ★★★
The most attractive place to stay in Pärnu, this attractive Art Nouveau hotel, built in 1905, has luxurious rooms and an excellent restaurant.
Mere 7, Pärnu.
Tel: (372) 447 3888.
www.ammende.ee

Scandic Rannahotell ★★
Built during Pärnu's pre-World War II heyday as a fashionable beach resort, this Art Deco-style building is a landmark on the town's beach and regarded as an architectural treasure, too. It offers good service and value for money and has an excellent restaurant and off-street parking, but rooms are small and some are in need of refurbishment.
Ranna 5.
Tel (372) 443 2950.
www.scandic-hotels.com

Aadu Tourist Farm ★
Simply charming family-run bed and breakfast accommodation in thatched log cabins (all with en-suite shower and WC) on a former farm. Set among wildflower meadows, it is close to the sea and around 16km (10 miles) from Kuressaare and its castle. This is an excellent base for exploring the island, and perfect for children.
Suure-Rootsi kula, Saaremaa.
Tel: (372) 509 3981.
www.aadutalu.ee

On business

English is almost universally spoken in Estonian business circles, along with German, Swedish and Finnish. Russian is rarely used in business.

Business centres offering secretarial and translation services, photocopying, internet and email access, personal computers and other facilities are available in all major hotels in Tallinn.

Bank accounts

Banks in Estonia are modern, secure and customer-friendly. Many major European and international banking institutions have Estonian branches, and most banking is in the hands of international institutions.

Hansapank
Liivalaia 8, Tallinn.
Tel: (372) 631 0310. www.hansa.ee

Krediidipank
Narva mantee 4, Tallinn.
Tel: (372) 669 0990.
www.krediidipank.ee

Business hours

Banks
Mon–Fri 10am–4pm.

Government and business offices
Mon–Fri 9am–5pm.

Business visas

Business visas are not required by British, Irish or other EU citizens, or by US, Canadian, Australian or New Zealand citizens.

Capital investment

Foreign investment has become even easier with the harmonisation of Estonia's legal system with EU norms. Contact the Estonian Investment Agency (*www.eia.ee*).

Chambers of Commerce

American Chamber of Commerce
Harju 6, Tallinn.
Tel: (372) 631 0522. www.acce.ee

British Estonian Chamber of Commerce
Dunkri 4, Tallinn.
Tel: (372) 566 6623. www.becc.ee

Estonian Chamber of Commerce
Toom-Kooli 17, Tallinn.
Tel: (372) 646 0244. www.koda.ee

Conference facilities

Estonian National Library Conference Centre
Tõnismägi 2, Tallinn.
Tel: (372) 630 7262. www.nlib.ee

Olümpia Conference Centre
Reval hotel Olümpia, Liivalaia 33.

Tel: (372) 631 5334.
www.revalhotels.com
Radisson SAS Hotel Tallinn
Ravala 3. Tel: (372) 682 3000.
www.radissonsas.com

Corruption

In the chaotic period immediately after independence, Estonia suffered from some dubious business practices. It has, however, made much greater progress than any other ex-Soviet republic in stamping out shady dealing.

Etiquette

Estonian business manners are straightforward to the point of bluntness, and meetings often take place outside business hours to save valuable time. Business in Estonia is still overwhelmingly male-dominated.

Government contracts

All government business is centred in Tallinn. Contracts are awarded by public tender and knowledgeable local representation is advisable.

Language

Translators and interpreters include:
A&A Lingua
Kreutzwaldi 12.
Tel: (372) 683 0321. www.lingua.ee

Legal firms

The legal system in Estonia is based on Continental European civil law and is closely modelled on the German legal system.

Hedman Osborne Clarke Alliance
Narva mantee 11d. Tel: (372) 611 6950.
www.hedman-attorneys.com
Hough, Hubner, Hutt and Partners
Viru 5, Tallinn. Tel: (372) 644 6227.
www.hough-hubner-attorneys.ee

Real estate

Those planning to invest in property should retain an Estonian lawyer (*see Legal firms, above*).
Brokers include:
Ober-Haus Real Estate
Narva mantee 53, Tallinn.
Tel: (372) 665 9700.
www.ober-haus.com
Mortgages are available through:
Baltic-American Mortgage Company
Roosikrantsi 11, Tallinn.
Tel: (372) 627 7180.
www.eluasamelaen.ee.

Residence and work permits

EU citizens can live and work in Estonia without residence and work permits for up to three months. In order to work in Estonia a non-EU citizen must hold a work permit.

Tax

Estonia has agreements on avoiding double taxation with 29 countries including EU countries. Companies are subject to Corporate Income Tax. Value Added Tax is a compulsory 18 per cent supplement to nearly all goods and services sold in Estonia. Social Tax is 33 per cent and includes social security tax and medical insurance.

Practical guide

Arriving

Visas are not required for British, Irish or other EU citizens. Holders of Australian, Canadian, New Zealand or US passports do not need a visa for stays of up to three months in a six-month period. South Africans require a visa, but holders of a South African passport may enter Estonia if they hold a visa for Latvia or Lithuania. Visitors may be required to prove that they have access to enough funds to support themselves for the length of their stay, based on a daily expenditure of 320 kroons.

By air

Tallinn International Airport is Estonia's main international airport and is located less than 5km (3 miles) from the city centre. The airport is compact and modern, with currency facilities, automatic teller machines (ATMs) and car rental desks located on the ground floor. A taxi to the city centre takes around five minutes, but Tallinn taxis are notorious for overcharging, so the fare should be confirmed before boarding. Bus 2 leaves from the arrivals hall every 30 minutes and takes less than 10 minutes to reach the Viru Hotel stop in the city centre. The fare is very cheap. Buy tickets from the driver.

Tallinn International Airport
Lennujaama 2. Tel: (372) 605 8888. www.tallinn-airport.ee

Estonian Air
Lennujaama tee 1. Tel: (372) 640 1163 (customer service). Airport ticket office tel: (372) 640 1161. www.estonian-air.ee

Tallinn's modern airport terminal

Avies Airlines
Tel: (372) 605 8022. www.avies.ee. Flies to Kuressaare (Saaremaa) from Gotland in Sweden.
Aero Airlines
Tel: (372) 611 0740. www.aeroairlines.com. Flies to Kuressaare from Helsinki.

By bus

Buses from western Europe, Scandinavia and Russia are the cheapest way of travelling to Estonia, but bus travel involves long and often uncomfortable journeys and must be booked weeks or even months in advance. Buses from the west arrive via Vilnius and Rīga at Tallinn's main bus station, about 1.6km (1 mile) south of the centre, but some services also stop next to the Viru hotel and shopping mall in central Tallinn. Buses 17 and 23 and trams 2 and 4 go from the bus station to the centre.
Central Bus Station
Lastedoku 46. Regional bus information: Tel: (372) 680 0900 or 680 0909.

Long-distance international buses from London to Estonia are operated by:
Eurolines
52 Grosvenor Gardens, London W1. Tel: 01582 404 511. www.eurolines.ee

By car

European Union citizens should hold the new European Driving Licence. Others require an International Driving Licence. All drivers entering Estonia with their own vehicle must have valid registration papers and proof of a valid insurance policy, such as the internationally recognised Green Card. This should be obtained from your insurer before departure.

By rail

It is possible to arrive in Estonia by train, travelling from western Europe via Poland, Lithuania and Latvia, and it is also possible to travel onward to Russia by rail. The daily Baltic Express operating between Warsaw in Poland and Tallinn (with a change of train at the Polish-Lithuanian border) takes around 17 hours and fares are very reasonable. Trains from Tallinn to St Petersburg in Russia take around ten hours, with at least two services daily. For up-to-date details of rail services, consult the *Thomas Cook European Rail Timetable* (published monthly, available from UK branches of Thomas Cook *tel: 01733 416477* or buy online at *www.thomascookpublishing.com*).

Tallinn's Baltic Station is only 180m (200yds) from the central Old Town and has modern facilities including a good restaurant, left-luggage storage, an exchange office and cash machines. Trams 1 or 2 from behind the station head into the city centre but taxis at the station are notorious for overcharging foreign visitors.
Tallinn Baltic Station
Toompuiestee 37.
Tel: (372) 615 6851 or 1447.
www.baltijaam.ee

By sea

Frequent ferries and high-speed catamarans arrive in Tallinn from Helsinki in Finland (3–4 hours by ferry, around 90 minutes by hydrofoil and less than 2 hours by catamaran) and from Stockholm in Sweden.

Ferry companies include:

Eckero Line
Tel: (372) 631 8606. www.eckeroline.ee

Lindaline
Tel: (372) 699 9333. www.lindaline.ee

Nordic Jet Line
Tel: (372) 613 7000. www.njl.info

SuperSeaCat
Tel: (372) 610 0000. www.superseacat.com

Tallink
Tel: (372) 640 9808. www.tallink.ee

Viking Line
Tel: (372) 666 3966. www.vikingline.ee

Tallinn Passenger Port has four terminals, with left-luggage facilities, a tourism information office (in the main hall of Terminal A), Bureaux de Change and cash machines.

The Passenger Port is less than 1.5km (1 mile) from the city centre.
Sadama 25. Tel: (372) 631 8550. www.portoftallinn.com.
Open: 7am–11pm.

Hydrofoils arrive at the Linnahall hydrofoil harbour.
Mere pst. 20. Tel: (372) 699 9333. www.lindaline.ee

Saaremaa Shipping Company sails between Kuressaare and Ventspils in Latvia, and to Sillamae from Kotka in Finland.
Tel: (372) 452 4350. www.laevakompanii.ee

Children

Children are accepted almost everywhere, although families with children will not find many of Tallinn's noisier bars suitable. Estonians do value politeness and have little tolerance for ill-behaved children. Children up to the age of ten are generally given half-price admission to most museums and attractions.

Climate

The best time to visit is between May and October, when the days are long and often sunny. Snow is usual from November until March. Late winter and

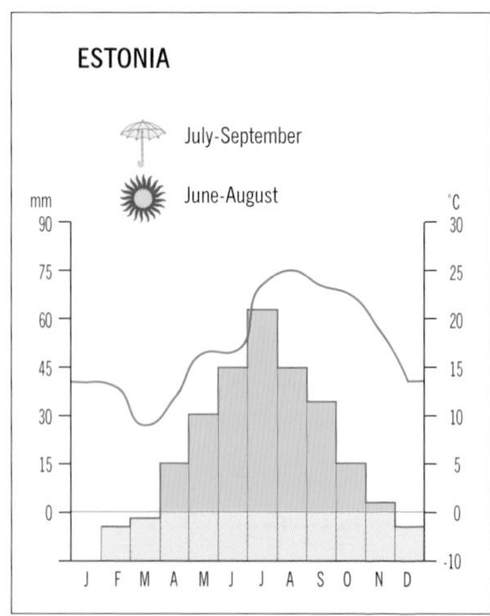

WEATHER CONVERSION CHART

25.4mm = 1 inch

°F = 1.8 × °C + 32

early spring, when snow melts into slush, are the least attractive times of year. February is the coldest month, with temperatures of –3.5°C to –7°C (19–26°F). July is the warmest, with temperatures of 16–20°C (61–68°F). In extreme conditions, winter temperatures can sink as low as –23°C (–9°F) and summer temperatures can rise to 30°C (86°F).

Crime

Tallinn's violent crime rate is no worse than most European capital cities, but tourists are often the victims of petty theft. Stay sober, and avoid unfamiliar areas of the city at night. Keep an eye on your belongings at all times. Do not leave valuables, travel documents or money in hotel rooms – carry as much as you need for the day and lock the rest in a hotel safe deposit or strongbox. Theft from cars is very common and thieves target foreign-registered vehicles and rental cars. Do not leave valuables in your car at any time. To report a crime, contact the **Tallinn central police station** (*Lootsi 15; tel: (372) 612 4210; for* **emergencies**: *tel: 110*).

Overcharging by taxi drivers (sometimes using a meter rigged to show a higher fare) is a common complaint.

Customs

Those entering from another European Union country may import (in theory) an unlimited amount of alcohol, tobacco and other goods for personal consumption.

CONVERSION TABLE

FROM	TO	MULTIPLY BY
Inches	Centimetres	2.54
Feet	Metres	0.3048
Yards	Metres	0.9144
Miles	Kilometres	1.6090
Acres	Hectares	0.4047
Gallons	Litres	4.5460
Ounces	Grams	28.35
Pounds	Grams	453.6
Pounds	Kilograms	0.4536
Tons	Tonnes	1.0160

To convert back, for example from centimetres to inches, divide by the number in the third column.

MEN'S SUITS

UK	36	38	40	42	44	46	48
Rest of Europe	46	48	50	52	54	56	58
USA	36	38	40	42	44	46	48

DRESS SIZES

UK	8	10	12	14	16	18
France	36	38	40	42	44	46
Italy	38	40	42	44	46	48
Rest of Europe	34	36	38	40	42	44
USA	6	8	10	12	14	16

MEN'S SHIRTS

UK	14	14.5	15	15.5	16	16.5	17
Rest of Europe	36	37	38	39/40	41	42	43
USA	14	14.5	15	15.5	16	16.5	17

MEN'S SHOES

UK	7	7.5	8.5	9.5	10.5	11
Rest of Europe	41	42	43	44	45	46
USA	8	8.5	9.5	10.5	11.5	12

WOMEN'S SHOES

UK	4.5	5	5.5	6	6.5	7
Rest of Europe	38	38	39	39	40	41
USA	6	6.5	7	7.5	8	8.5

Estonian roads are generally well surfaced and uncrowded

Guideline amounts are: 90 litres of wine; 110 litres of beer, 10 litres of spirits (21 per cent alcohol or more); 800 cigarettes, 400 cigarillos, 200 cigars and 1kg of pure tobacco.

Arrivals from non EU countries may bring in two litres of wine, three litres of spirits, 200 cigarettes or 100 cigarillos or 50 cigars or 250g pure tobacco.

Those entering or leaving Estonia with currency exceeding 15,000 euros must declare it to Estonian Customs. *Contact: Customs Department, Lõkke 5. Tel: (372) 683 5700. www.customs.ee*

Driving

Car hire

Most major international car rental companies now have branches in Tallinn. Car rental is up to 50 per cent more expensive than the European average and around twice as expensive as in the US. Drivers must be over 21 and have a valid driving licence from their own country. Traffic drives on the right. Headlights must be switched on when driving on highways even during daylight.

It is illegal to drink and drive (the legal blood/alcohol limit is 0.002 per cent, effectively zero).

Emergency

Estonia does not have an automobile club or motorists' association. In emergencies, call the general police emergency number *110* or *02*.

Insurance

Travellers to Estonia should purchase a comprehensive personal travel insurance policy (available from travel agencies, tour operators, home and life insurance companies, credit card companies and banks) before leaving home. It should give adequate cover for medical expenses and emergency medical evacuation, loss and theft of valuables and money, and expenses incurred due to cancellation or delays.

Liability arising from motor accidents is not usually included; this is normally included in your motor insurance policy (if taking your own car) or in the policies offered at point of rental by car hire companies.

Motorists driving their own cars should extend their policy to cover theft, accidental damage and liability to include Estonia and points en route and get a Green Card from their home insurer as proof of third-party liability cover.

If hiring a car, it is advisable to pay the additional fee for the rental company's collision damage waiver (CDW) which is usually paid at the time of rental. Most CDW policies include a set excess limit and hold drivers responsible for any damage repairs or liability costing less than this level. Major international car rental companies also offer drivers additional liability cover.

You should personally check details of exclusions and details of cover to ensure that the amount of cover is adequate.

Petrol

Leaded, unleaded and diesel fuel is readily available at fuel stations throughout Estonia and costs around the European average. Rental cars use only unleaded fuel. Filling stations in rural areas often prefer cash to credit cards. Estonia is a small country, distances are short and there is little risk of running out of fuel.

Roads

Estonian roads are relatively good, but most of the highway network is two-lane only and surfaces in country areas may be potholed. Snow, ice and darkness make driving riskier and more stressful in winter.

Speed limits

Speed limits in built-up areas are 50kph (approximately 30mph), and on highways the maximum speed is 110kph (approximately 70mph).

Electricity

220 volts AC, 50Hz. European plugs work in most sockets in modern buildings, but a few older buildings still use the thinner-pinned Soviet version. Those planning to stay in older hotels, country guesthouses or private homes should carry spare batteries for accessories such as mobile phones or cameras or make sure they are fully charged beforehand, as converters for old-fashioned Russian sockets are hard to find.

Embassies and consulates

All embassies and consulates are in Tallinn.

Canada *Toom-Kooli 13, 2nd floor. Tel: (372) 627 3311. www.canada.ee*

Ireland *Vene 2, 2nd floor. Tel: (372) 681 1888. embassytallinn@eircom.net*

United Kingdom *Wismari 6. Tel: (372) 667 4700. www.britishembassy.gov.uk*

USA *Kentmanni 20.*
Tel: (372) 668 8100. wwwusemb.ee

Emergency telephone numbers

Ambulance *112*
Police *110*
Fire *112*

Health

There are no mandatory vaccination requirements, and travel to Estonia poses no special health risks. Tap water can be drunk without adverse effects, but ageing water pipes in older buildings sometimes give discoloured water. Estonia has reciprocal health care arrangements with the UK and Ireland as fellow members of the EU. This entitles visitors only to the minimal level of state-provided health care in Estonia. State-run hospitals are poorly equipped, and visitors should obtain a private health insurance policy, with a level of cover that includes repatriation under medical supervision in emergencies before they arrive. Estonia has made great progress in dealing with its pollution problems, but some untreated sewage is still discharged into the Baltic. Visitors should take local advice before going into the sea close to towns and cities.

Getting around Tallinn by trishaw

Media

English-language newspapers including the *International Herald Tribune, USA Today* and most British national newspapers are on sale in Tallinn on the day of publication or on the following day. Leading news magazines such as *Time*, *Newsweek* and the *Economist*, as well as a range of leisure and special interest magazines in English, are also readily available immediately on publication. Outside the capital, foreign publications are less easy to find.

Estonia and its Baltic neighbours have also spawned a number of home-grown English-language titles, notably the newspaper *Baltic Paper* (see also its website, *www.balticsww.com*, for news and opinions from Estonia, Latvia and Lithuania) and the always useful and entertaining listings magazine, *Tallinn in your Pocket* which also has an indispensably helpful website, *www.inyourpocket.com.*

Most hotels above three-star standard offer satellite TV giving access to English-language channels such as BBC World, CNN, MTV and other major satellite services.

Internet access is easy to find, with cybercafés and internet centres in Tallinn and in all regional towns. Tallinn

Language

Estonian is a Finno-Ugrian language, closely related to Finnish and more distantly related to Magyar. It is written in the Roman alphabet, with numerous diacritical marks indicating peculiarly Estonian pronunciations of certain letters.

GREETINGS AND COURTESIES

Hello	Tere
Goodbye	Head aega
Good morning	Tere hommikust
Good evening	Tere õhtust
Good night	Head ööd
Please	Palun
Thank you	Tänan

EVERYDAY EXPRESSIONS

Yes	Jah
No	Ei
There is	Ole
There is not	Ei ole
How much?	Kui palju?
Expensive	Kallis
Cheap	Odav

DAYS OF THE WEEK

Sunday	Pühapäev
Monday	Esmaspäev
Tuesday	Teisipäev
Wednesday	Lomapäev
Thursday	Neljpäev
Friday	Reede
Saturday	Laupäev

TIME

Today	Täna
Yesterday	Eile
Tomorrow	Homme

NUMBERS

One	Üks
Two	Kaks
Three	Kolm
Four	Neli
Five	Viis
Six	Kuus
Seven	Seitse
Eight	Kaheksa
Nine	Üheksa
Ten	Kümme
Eleven	Üsteist
Twelve	Kaksteist
Thirteen	Kolmteist
Fourteen	Neliteist
Fifteen	Viisteist
Sixteen	Kuusteist
Seventeen	Seitseteist
Eighteen	Kaheksateist
Nineteen	Üheksateist
Twenty	Kaksümmend
Thirty	Kolmkümmend
Forty	Nelikümmend
Fifty	Viiskümmend
Sixty	Kuuskümmend
Seventy	Seitsekümmend
Eighty	Kaheksakümmend
Ninety	Üheksakümmend
One hundred	Sada

generally has good broadband access; access from smaller towns can be slower.

Money matters

Estonia's national currency, the kroon (pronounced 'crone'), replaced the Soviet rouble shortly after independence, and is due to be replaced by the euro (the main EU currency) sometime after 2007.

The kroon (EEK) is pegged to the euro at €1 to EEK 15.65. The euro is not officially legal currency in Estonia but is increasingly widely accepted in international hotels and upmarket shops.

Kroon currency notes are issued in denominations of EEK 2, 5, 10, 25, 50, 100 and 500. Coins are issued in denominations of EEK1 and EEK5, and coins of 10, 20 and 50 senti (cents) are also in circulation, although they are almost worthless.

Holders of major credit and debit cards can easily withdraw cash from automatic teller machines (ATMs) in Tallinn and provincial cities. Most hotels, restaurants and larger shops accept Visa and MasterCard credit cards. American Express and Diners' Club cards are less widely accepted. Banks offer cash advances on credit cards, usually for a 1 per cent fee, and Thomas Cook and American Express traveller's cheques in euros, US dollars or sterling can be exchanged at most banks. Australian, Canadian and NZ dollars and South African rands may be less easy to exchange.

Branches of the Krediidipank and main post offices also handle Western Union wire transfers.

National holidays

Estonia shares most of its national holidays with the rest of Europe. Independence Day celebrates the first declaration of independence in 1918, while Victory Day marks the expulsion of the last foreign invaders from the Baltic states in 1919, and the Day of Restoration of Independence marks the country's breakaway from the USSR. St John's Day, on 24 June, is a midsummer celebration.

1 January New Year's Day
24 February Independence Day
March/April Good Friday
March/April Easter Sunday
1 May May Day
9 May Mother's Day
23 June Victory Day

Kuressaare's St Nicholas Church

24 June St John's Day
20 August Day of Restoration of Independence
25 December Christmas Day
26 December Boxing Day

Government offices, banks and many businesses close on these days, but except for Christmas Day, Boxing Day and New Year's Day most shops, bars, restaurants and museums stay open.

Opening hours

Banks
Mon–Fri 10am–4pm.
Government and business offices
Mon–Fri 9am–5pm.
Museums
Opening hours vary widely.
Shops
Mon–Fri 10am–6pm, Sat 10am–5pm. Closed: Sun.

Organised tours

UK-based Baltic Holidays is the leading specialist holiday company offering tailor-made package holidays to Estonia (and its neighbours). The company offers beach and island holidays, escorted coach tours and activity holidays.
40 Princess Street, Manchester. Tel: 0845 070 5711. www.balticholidays.com

Other tour companies based in Estonia include Tallinn-based Travel to Baltics which offers sightseeing tours in Tallinn, escorted coach tours, and accommodation deals throughout Estonia.
Tel: (372) 610 8616. www.travel2baltics.com

Pharmacies

Pharmacies in Estonia are well qualified and adequately stocked with essential medicines, most of which can be bought without a prescription. Normal opening hours are: *Mon–Fri 10am–6pm, Sat 10am–5pm.* There is a 24-hour pharmacy in Tallinn (*Linnaapteek; tel: (372) 644 0244*).

Places of worship

Services in English are held every Sunday at 3pm in Tallinn's Church of the Holy Ghost. Tallinn also has several other Lutheran churches, several of which also hold services in English, as well as a Russian Orthodox cathedral. Elsewhere, there are relatively few places of worship in Estonia.

Police

Estonia has no dedicated tourist police force and not all police officers speak English; however, they are usually efficient and helpful when dealing with foreigners. Paperwork in the event of theft or accidents can be time-consuming.

Post offices

The Central Post Office in Tallinn is at *Narva mantee 1. Tel: (372) 661 6616. Open: Mon–Fri 7.30am–8pm & Sat 9am–6pm.*
Other post offices are normally open: *weekdays 9am–6pm & Sat 9.30am–3pm.*

A letter takes one to three days to arrive within Baltic and Nordic countries and up to a week to other destinations.

Public transport

Timetables

For up-to-date details of train, ferry and long-distance bus services consult the *Thomas Cook European Rail Timetable* (published monthly), available to buy online at *www.thomascookpublishing.com*, or from UK branches of Thomas Cook *tel: 01733 416477.*

By air

There are regular flights between Tallinn and Hiiumaa and Saaremaa. Tartu also has an international airport.

By bus

Estonia has an efficient network of bus services connecting Tallinn with provincial towns and cities and operated by competing, privately run bus companies. Express coaches are more comfortable than local services. Tickets should be bought from the main bus station at least two hours in advance. *Express Hotline tel: 1182.*

By ferry

Ferries connect Estonia's islands with mainland ports, including Pirita, Paldiski, Haapsalu and Pärnu.

By taxi

Taxis in Tallinn are notorious for overcharging Estonians and foreign visitors alike. Always agree on an approximate fare before boarding. It is not advisable to share taxis with strangers.

By train

The Estonian Railways network covers all main towns and smaller villages. Most trains are one-class, but trains to Tartu and on the line to Valga offer two-class seating. The Moscow Express train from Tallinn to Moscow (taking 16 hours) has first-class sleeping compartments.

Student and youth travel

Holders of the internationally recognised ISIC student card are entitled to discounts on public transport and in selected restaurants and hostels. A valid student ID card normally entitles visitors to reduced admission to museums and other attractions.

Sustainable tourism

Thomas Cook is a strong advocate of ethical and fairly traded tourism and believes that the travel experience should be as good for the places visited as it is for the people that visit. That's why we're a firm supporter of The Travel Foundation, a charity that develops solutions to help improve and protect holiday destinations, their environment, traditions and culture. To find out what you can do to make a positive difference to the places you travel to and the people who live there, please visit *www.thetravelfoundation.org.uk*

Telephone

Emergency ambulance services: *112*
Directory enquiries: *1182* or *1188*
Long-distance information: *1188*
Operator: *16 115*
Reversed charge calls: *16 116*

Public phone booths use a card system. Cards are sold at street kiosks and in hotels and cost EEK 30, EEK 50 or EEK 100. City codes were phased out in 2004. To call any number in Estonia from abroad, dial (*00 372*). To call abroad from Estonia dial 00 plus the relevant country code:
Australia *61*
Canada *1*
Ireland *353*
New Zealand *64*
UK *44*
USA *1*

Time

Estonia operates Greenwich Mean Time + 2 hours.

Tipping

A tip of ten per cent is sufficient in restaurants. Gratuities are also welcomed by hotel porters and taxi drivers. Tipping is not necessary in bars or self-service restaurants.

Tourist offices

Tourist offices have improved enormously since the end of the Soviet-era and there are helpful tourist information offices in all Estonian towns with a good supply of maps and information brochures in English. Most information offices also offer an accommodation booking service, and all have helpful, English-speaking staff. Estonia has no tourist offices outside Estonia. In the UK, USA and Canada, Estonian embassies can supply tourism brochures.
Canada *260 Dalhousie Street, Suite 210, Ottawa. Tel: (1) 613 789 4222. email: embassy.ottawa@mfa.ee.*
UK *16 Hyde Park Gate, London SW7 5DG. Tel: (44) 020 7589 3428. www.estonia.gov.uk. email: embassy.london@estonia.gov.uk.*
USA *2131 Massachusetts Ave, Washington DC 2000. Tel: (01) 202 588 0101. email: info@estemb.org*

Travellers with disabilities

Facilities in Estonia for travellers with disabilities are limited, but are improving. Newer hotels have lifts large enough for wheelchair users, and some have rooms with bathrooms designed for wheelchair users. New restaurants and cafés, however, have toilets with wheelchair access. Museums and art galleries do not yet have induction-loop facilities for people with hearing aids.

More information for travellers with disabilities, including wheelchair users and people with impaired sight and hearing, is available (in English) from the website of the Estonian Chamber for Disabled People: *www.epikoda.ee*

Index

Acknowledgements

Thomas Cook wishes to thank ROBIN McKELVIE for the photographs in this book, to whom copyright belongs, except for the following images:

ALATSKIVI CASTLE: page 88; EDUARD VILDE MUUSEUM: page 45; ESTONIAN NATIONAL OPERA: page 155; ESTONIAN RAILWAY MUSEUM: page 117; ESTONIAN TOURIST BOARD: pages 5, 60, 78, 147, 170; JAAK NILSON PHOTOSTOCK: pages 27, 96; MIKE PRINCE: page 111a; NATIONAL MUSEUM OF ESTONIA: pages 72, 97; OLDE HANSA: page 167; OTTO PFISTER: page 111b; PICTURES COLOUR LIBRARY: page 173; PIRITA TOP SPA: page 55; ROBIN GAULDIE: pages 8, 16, 17, 21, 23, 29, 58, 59, 61, 62, 85, 90, 102, 109, 121, 122, 126, 134, 136, 137, 178, 182, 184, 186; SA VIRUMAA MUUSEUMID: pages 66, 68; STATE FOREST MANAGEMENT, JÜRI PERE: pages 140, 141; TALLINNA LAULUVÄLJAK (KATRIN OJA): page 24; TARTU AVIATION MUSEUM: page 91; VAIKE-MAARJA MUSEUM: page 70; WIKIMEDIA COMMONS: pages 54 (SM), 79, 119 (HendrixEesti), 133 (Maurycy Gottlieb); WORLD PICTURES/PHOTOSHOT: pages 1, 9, 19, 33, 40, 46, 69, 125, 144, 149, 151, 160, 161, 165.

For CAMBRIDGE PUBLISHING MANAGEMENT LIMITED:
Project editor: Karen Beaulah
Typesetter: Paul Queripel
Proofreader: Jan McCann
Indexer: Karolin Thomas

SEND YOUR THOUGHTS TO BOOKS@THOMASCOOK.COM

We're committed to providing the very best up-to-date information in our travel guides and constantly strive to make them as useful as they can be. You can help us to improve future editions by letting us have your feedback. If you've made a wonderful discovery on your travels that we don't already feature, if you'd like to inform us about recent changes to anything that we do include, or if you simply want to let us know your thoughts about this guidebook and how we can make it even better – we'd love to hear from you.

Send us ideas, discoveries and recommendations today and then look out for your valuable input in the next edition of this title.

Emails to the above address, or letters to Travellers Series Editor, Thomas Cook Publishing, PO Box 227, Coningsby Road, Peterborough PE3 8SB, UK.

Please don't forget to let us know which title your feedback refers to!